MYTHS AND MYSTERIES

OF

ILLINOIS

MYTHS AND MYSTERIES SERIES

MYTHS AND MYSTERIES

OF
ILLINOIS

TRUE STORIES
OF THE UNSOLVED AND UNEXPLAINED

RICHARD MORENO

Guilford, Connecticut

Copyright © 2013 by Morris Book Publishing, LLC

Map by Alena Joy Pearce © Morris Book Publishing, LLC
Project editor: Lauren Szalkiewicz
Layout: Justin Pospisil-Marciano

Library of Congress Cataloging-in-Publication Data is available on file.

ISBN 978-0-7627-7827-0

Printed in the United States of America

10 9 8 7 6 5 4 3 2 1

CONTENTS

Introduction vii

Chapter 1:   The Gasman Cometh 1

Chapter 2:   Big Bird on the Loose 14

Chapter 3:   Macomb's Firebug 27

Chapter 4:   Tragedy in the Suburbs 41

Chapter 5:   Burning Mysteries 54

Chapter 6:   Mary, Mary, Quite Contrary 65

Chapter 7:   The Horror 77

Chapter 8:   Accidental Shooting or Assassination? 86

Chapter 9:   Possession in Watseka 99

Chapter 10:   Invasion of the Phantom Gasbags 111

Chapter 11:   Did Anyone Really Starve on Starved Rock? 125

Chapter 12:   The New Monster of the Midway 137

Chapter 13:   Virgil Ball's Obsession 146

Chapter 14:   The Diabolical Dr. Holmes 158

Bibliography 175

Index 194

About the Author 200

IOWA

WISCONSIN

Lake Koshkonong

Pell Lake

Lake Michigan

Mississippi River

Rock River

Iowa River

CHICAGO ○

ILLINOIS

OTTAWA ○

Senachwine Lake

WATSEKA ○

○ MACOMB

○ NORMAL
○ BLOOMINGTON

ASTORIA ○

LAWNDALE ○

Illinois River

SPRINGFIELD ✪

Lake Springfield

Sangchris Lake

Lake Shelbyville

○ MATTOON

Wabash River

Mississippi River

MISSOURI

ALTON ○

Missouri River

Carlyle Lake

Gasconade River

Meramec River

Rend Lake

○ ENFIELD

INDIANA

Green River

KENTUCKY

N

Ohio River

Lake Wappapello

LAKE
Barkley

100 KILOMETERS

50   100 MILES

Kentucky Lake

ARKANSAS

TENNESSEE

INTRODUCTION

Edgar Allan Poe once wrote, "There was much of the beautiful, much of the wanton, much of the bizarre, something of the terrible, and not a little of that which might have excited disgust." He wasn't describing Illinois—but he could have been. When it comes to subjects strange and mysterious, Illinois is fertile ground. It's a place where monsters are both real (e.g., serial killers Richard Speck, John Wayne Gacy, Dr. H. H. Holmes) and perhaps imaginary (e.g., Bigfoot, mud monsters, Mothman).

In the course of writing this book, it became abundantly clear to me that over the past 300-plus years—beginning when explorers Louis Jolliet and Jacques Marquette became the first non-Indians to set foot in Illinois—some pretty strange stuff has happened in the state. And that's what has made writing this book so enjoyable. Illinois tales, legends, myths, and mysteries make it such a fascinating place to live. When I moved to the rural western Illinois community of Macomb about five years ago, I had no idea that one of the truly unexplained "Firestarter" mysteries—the so-called Macomb Poltergeist, which I included in this book—happened just a few miles away from where I live. Nor had I ever heard of the "Watseka Wonder," one of the first cases of spiritual possession in America, or known of the "Enfield

Horror," a bizarre story involving a three-legged, leaping, smelly pink-eyed monster. I knew nothing of the Mattoon Gasser, Thunderbirds, Resurrection Mary, or spontaneous human combustion. Nor did I know many of the sad and tragic details of the horrendous and still unsolved crimes mentioned in this book.

Is everything in this book real? I don't know. I like to think that every source cited in this book was sincere and telling the truth—or at least the truth as he or she believed it. In the end maybe the stories that seem just a little too fantastical or a bit unbelievable are simply examples of the phenomenon known as mass hysteria—which would certainly explain how Rod Blagojevich was able to get elected governor of the state—twice.

* * *

I would like to thank several folks who helped me with this book, including Kathy Nichols, archives specialist, Special Collections, Western Illinois University; N. Adam Watson, photographic archivist, State Archives of Florida; and Heather Moore, photo historian, US Senate Historical Office.

And finally, I would like to dedicate this book to my daughter, Julia, who read each chapter and offered valuable suggestions and advice. This one is for you, Boo.

Richard Moreno
Macomb, Illinois
October 2012

CHAPTER 1

The Gasman Cometh

Someone terrified a large number of people in the eastern Illinois community of Mattoon in late August and early September 1944. To this day no one is quite sure who it was or how it was done—or exactly what occurred. Local newspapers named the unknown perpetrator the "Anesthetic Prowler," the "Mad Anesthetist," and finally, the "Mad Gasser of Mattoon."

For almost two weeks the approximately 16,000 residents of Mattoon were filled with anxiety; some refused to even stay in their homes for fear of being visited by the shadowy assailant (or assailants!) who allegedly used a sweet-smelling paralyzing gas that made people sick. There were even reports of a mysterious black-clad figure running through the affected neighborhoods. Local police, aided by the state police and the FBI, scrambled for an explanation or even a whiff of a perpetrator.

Then, almost as suddenly as the attacks started, they were over. Mattoon police chief C. E. Cole quickly dismissed the entire series of events, saying the initial citizen complaints had been triggered by strong odor emissions from nearby industrial plants, which were then exaggerated by the media and a hysterical public.

A University of Illinois psychology student, Donald M. Johnson, visited the community about a month after things quieted and wrote an article that appeared the following January in the prestigious *Journal of Abnormal and Social Psychology*. In the article, Johnson concluded that "the case of the 'phantom anesthetist' was entirely psychogenic."

According to Johnson, hysteria—not a mystery gas—caused the paralysis some had experienced. "As the news spread, other people reported similar symptoms, more exciting stories were written, and so the affair snowballed," he wrote.

Johnson's paper became one of the seminal works on the subject of mass hysteria and has been cited in dozens of subsequent scholarly papers as proof of the phenomenon.

So what really happened between August 31 and September 11, 1944, in Mattoon? The first news story indicating anything was amiss appeared in a front-page story in the September 2 issue of the *Mattoon Daily Journal-Gazette* headlined, "'Anesthetic Prowler' on Loose," with a remarkably prescient subhead that said, "Mrs. Kearney and Daughter First Victims." The subhead implied that there would be other victims—and there were.

According to the story the prowler utilized some type of anesthetic gas to overpower Aline Kearney and her three-year-old daughter, Dorothy.

"It was shortly after 11 o'clock Friday night when I went to bed, taking with me my daughter, Dorothy," she told the newspaper. "I first noticed a sickening, sweet odor in the bedroom, but at the time thought it might be from flowers outside the window. However, the odor grew stronger and I began to feel a paralysis of my legs and lower body."

Aline Kearney said her throat became extremely dry and her lips started to burn. The fumes were so strong they made her daughter begin to cough. Frightened and confused, she screamed for her sister, Martha Reedy, who was in the living room. Reedy entered the bedroom and immediately smelled the weird odor. She ran next door to the home of Mrs. Earl Robertson and asked her to call the police. The two women

PHOTO BY RICHARD MORENO

This two-story home at 1408 Marshall Street in Mattoon, Illinois, was the location of the first reported attack by the Mattoon Gasser.

returned to Aline Kearney's bedroom while Mr. Robertson searched the area around the house but found nothing. Police quickly arrived and also found no evidence of a prowler or explanation for Aline Kearney's sudden paralysis, which lasted for about a half hour.

Around midnight Aline Kearney's husband, who was working the night shift as a cab driver, received word that he needed to come home quickly. He arrived at the house, located at 1408 Marshall, at about twelve thirty in the morning to find a figure dressed in black clothing, head covered by a tight-fitting cap, standing outside the bedroom window.

Mr. Kearney jumped out of his car and chased the black figure, but the person escaped. He returned to his house to check on his family and called the police, who once again performed a thorough search of the area but found nothing.

"Opinions differ as to the type of anesthetic used. However, because of the odor, it was believed to have been chloroform or ether or a combination of both," the local newspaper speculated. "The ingredients could have been sprayed into the room in a fine mist and if used at a distance not too far from the sleepers would have proved effective, it was said."

In the newspaper's account, the Kearneys had "considerable sums of money" in the house at the time, which Aline Kearney was believed to have been counting in plain sight. The story ended by noting that the Kearney family temporarily moved in with a relative in another part of the city.

Interestingly, while the Kearney encounter was the first attack reported in the press, it was not the first to occur in Mattoon. A day earlier Mr. and Mrs. Urban Raef, who lived at 1817 Grant Avenue, smelled a strange, nauseating odor in their home on the morning of August 31.

Overcome by the smell and feeling too sick to get out of bed, Mr. Raef asked his wife to check the pilot light on the couple's stove, thinking the odor was the result of leaking gas. But when she tried to climb out of bed, she found she could not move her legs.

According to Scott Maruna, author of *The Mad Gasser of Mattoon*, a study of the events, the paralysis soon faded but was followed by vomiting. After nearly an hour the couple finally regained the ability to move and stumbled out of their bedroom. Bizarrely, the mysterious odor did not affect visiting friends who had stayed in another bedroom in the house.

Maruna said that since they could find no explanation for their temporary illness, the Raefs assumed it was the result of eating bad hot dogs the night before and did not report their experience to police until after they learned of the attack on the Kearney family.

There were a couple more episodes in the same Mattoon neighborhood on the night of September 1—in fact, the four residences that reported smelling the sickening gas on August 31 and September 1 were all within eight blocks of each other.

According to Maruna, shortly after the Kearney experience, several members of the Rider family, who lived at 2508 Prairie Avenue, reported a strange, sickening smell.

Mrs. Charles Rider (also called Mrs. George Rider in some accounts) said she detected an unusual scent that made her two children, Joe and Ann Marie, feel sick to their stomachs and restless. She said the odor was so strong it made her light-headed and she vomited.

In addition another family, unnamed in reports but living directly west of the Rider family, said they were awakened by a strange, sweet odor in their house that caused their children to vomit.

No further gas encounters occurred for the next three days. However, at about ten o'clock on the night of September 5, Beulah and Carl Cordes, who lived at 921 North 21st Street, arrived home and found a white salt sack on their front porch that sickened Mrs. Cordes after she sniffed it.

"Mrs. Cordes as a result of her experience with the 'drug' or 'anesthetic' was violently ill for more than two hours," the *Mattoon Daily Journal-Gazette* reported the next day. "Her throat and her mouth were so badly burned by the fumes she inhaled that blood came from cracks in her parched and swollen lips and her seared throat and the roof of her mouth."

The newspaper noted that in addition to the damp sack, the Cordes had found a worn skeleton key and a large, nearly empty lipstick tube at the edge of the front porch. Police sent the soaked cloth to the Illinois State Police Laboratory to be analyzed, but because the lab did not test it for nearly three days, it could not determine what chemicals had been used on the material.

The *Chicago Tribune*, which had now picked up on the story, said that police theorized the prowler might have been trying to enter the house when the Cordes family returned home and "dropped these articles in flight."

The Mattoon paper did note that shortly after the incident, police had picked up a man about a block from the Cordes's home for questioning, but he was released. According to the paper, "The man told police that he was 'lost.'" In his book, a skeptical Maruna wrote, "I spent my entire youth living within 10 miles of Mattoon. Knowing this town well, I find it very difficult to picture someone wandering around this small community 'lost.'"

The apparent reappearance of the anesthetic prowler forced the local police, who previously had considered the reports as the work of a burglar who perhaps was using chloroform, to turn to the Illinois Department of Public Safety and the FBI for assistance. Soon local police, off-duty police officers, and even armed local citizens were patrolling Mattoon's streets at night.

Despite the increased vigilance, the prowler struck again. On the evening of September 6, people living in seven different homes reported close encounters of the anesthetic kind.

For instance, at about ten o'clock, Laura Junkin, who lived in an apartment in the back of a restaurant at 821 Richmond Avenue, said she smelled something reminiscent of "cheap perfume" coming through one of her windows and began to feel woozy. She said her legs grew weak and she felt as if she could no longer move them.

Shortly after, eleven-year-old Glenda Henderschott, who was sleeping in her home at 612 South 14th Street, awoke feeling sick to her stomach. Two hours earlier her parents had telephoned police to say they had spotted a suspicious person near her window.

The next day, newspapers throughout the country contained wire service articles about Mattoon's "Poison Spray Prowler," as the suspected assailant was called in a headline in Florida's *St. Petersburg Times.*

The Associated Press reported that a mysterious "poison gas" had been sprayed through open bedroom windows that had "prostrated nine persons in four days." The United Press said a phantom prowler called the "Madman of Mattoon" had stalked the community for several days using a "gardenia" gas to anesthetize more than a dozen people in their beds.

The *Chicago Tribune* quoted police chief C. E. Cole as saying his entire department was on twenty-four-hour duty throughout the affected neighborhoods to capture the mystery gasser. In many of the articles, victims claimed they saw a tall, thin person dressed in black and wearing a close-fitting black skullcap prowling around their homes prior to or following a gas attack.

Reports continued to waft in over the next few days. On the evening of September 7, the gasser struck several times at the home of Frances Smith, principal of Columbia Grade School, and her sister, Maxine. The two told police that they had smelled a strange flowery odor in the house that caused them to cough and choke violently. They also experienced numbness in their arms and legs, which made it difficult to stand or walk.

Unable to move, they said they actually saw a second helping of the gas, which they described as a blue-colored mist, coming through the windows. The gasser returned to spray their house again on September 8 and September 10.

Not surprisingly, the fact that police—who were being heavily criticized for not stopping the attacks—could not come up with an assailant or explanation put the entire community on edge.

On September 8, the "Gas Fiend," as the *Chicago Tribune* now called the alleged gas-gushing prowler, hit the home of Mrs. Violet Driskell and her eleven-year-old daughter, Ramona.

The paper's description of the attack was familiar:

Eleven year old Ramona Driskell fled from her home when she and her mother, Mrs. Violet Driskell, were roused by a prowler, who, they said, attempted to remove a storm sash from their bedroom window. The girl said the fumes assailed her and made her ill as she stood on the porch, calling for help. Mrs. Driskell said she believed she saw the man run away.

By September 10, the United Press was reporting that the Mad Gasser had victimized twenty-five people in Mattoon. At the same time, investigators found no traces of chemicals on the sack picked up by Mrs. Cordes. The United Press said Richard T. Piper, superintendent of the state Bureau of Criminal Identification and

Investigation, reported that an analysis indicated it was nothing more than an empty salt sack. Stating the obvious, the story added: "'This,' Piper said, 'makes it more mysterious than ever.'"

Interestingly, about this time, newspaper stories also began expressing doubts about the very existence of the mystery gasman.

"Nearly all of the phantom's victims have been women and children and skeptics have advanced the theory that Mattoon's mad scientist is an imaginary character born in the comic books," noted the United Press. Investigator Piper, however, told the wire service he was convinced "there is a real boogie man." He hypothesized that it might be "an insane chemist, who delights in frightening his victims without causing them any permanent harm."

The last reported incident happened on the morning of September 11 when Bertha Bence, a fifty-four-year-old widow, said her bedroom suddenly filled with a sweet- smelling gas that caused her to nearly faint.

She yelled for help, which awoke her sons, who ran outside and spotted what they described as a short, heavy-set figure dressed in dark clothing running away from the house. Unable to catch the person, they returned to the house and spotted footprints in the flowerbed outside of their mother's bedroom. The prints appeared to have been made by someone wearing a pair of woman's thick-heeled work shoes.

And with that the tone of the media reports suddenly shifted, as law enforcement decided that all of the sightings were the result of overactive imaginations—primarily by hysterical women. (Most able-bodied local men were away, serving their country in World War II.)

Chief Cole told reporters that the initial reports of a sweet-smelling, paralyzing gas were most likely the result of winds blowing chemical fumes from a local industrial plant into the neighborhood. He suggested that a local plant manufactured fire extinguishers that used carbon tetrachloride, a gas that could have caused the temporary paralysis. The plant's manager, however, vocally denied the allegations, noting that none of the plant workers had ever had any symptoms like the gassing victims and the quantities of the gas maintained at the plant were far too small to affect people in the ways they reported.

On September 13 the *Chicago Tribune* offered the new official version of events. According to Police Commissioner Thomas V. Wright, the whole affair was nothing more than "fear induced by imagination."

But was it? According to Scott Maruna, many old-time Mattoon residents believe there was an intruder who was gassing their friends and neighbors—and they claim to know his identity.

Following interviews with dozens of longtime residents, Maruna believes the culprit was a local man named Farley Llewellyn. "Farley was the Mad Gasser of Mattoon," he said. "A large portion of Mattoon's current over-eighty population knew, and knows, that Farley was responsible for the gassings."

Maruna described Llewellyn as a brilliant but troubled man in his early thirties who had majored in chemistry at the

University of Illinois at Urbana-Champaign and maintained a well-equipped chemical laboratory in the trailer in which he lived. His father was a prominent member of the community who owned a local grocery store at 920 DeWitt Avenue.

According to Maruna, Llewellyn was a homosexual and thus was most likely bullied while growing up in Mattoon. He also drank too much and was emotionally unstable. Apparently Llewellyn was considered a credible suspect, as a few days after the first attack he was interviewed by police and placed under constant surveillance.

Yet despite being watched, Llewellyn was never spotted doing anything suspicious. Maruna's theory of what happened is that Llewellyn most likely committed the first three attacks, all, not coincidentally, against former high school classmates. The later gassings were the work of Llewellyn's sisters, who were trying to cover for their brother after police had made him a prime suspect.

As for the mystery gas, Maruna, a chemistry teacher, speculated that it would have been child's play for a gifted chemist like Llewellyn to concoct something like nitromethane, a fragrant gas capable of causing paralysis, burning and irritation to the mouth and nose, swelling of the lips, and the other reactions reported by victims. The gas remains potent for sixteen days—about the length of time that the gasser was active—and is highly explosive.

In fact a few days before the attacks began, there had been an explosion in Llewellyn's home/lab (located behind the family grocery store), which might have been his initial attempt to make a batch of the chemical. Maruna believes Llewellyn was not try-ing to make the victims sick but wanted to blow them up.

A postscript to the story: On September 11 Llewellyn's family quietly had him placed in a state mental hospital, where he remained for the rest of his life.

Of course not everyone agrees with Maruna's conclusions. In a rebuttal to Maruna's book that appeared in the *Illinois Times* in 2003, Robert Ladendorf, who coauthored a 2002 article in *Skeptical Inquirer* magazine titled, "The Mad Gasser of Mat-toon: How the Press Created an Imaginary Chemical Weapons Attack," questioned Maruna's assumptions and evidence, which he said were highly speculative.

Ladendorf concluded that "mass hysteria or psychogenic illness, thus remains as the most likely cause of the two-week inci-dent in Mattoon in 1944, not Farley Llewellyn and his sisters."

In the end the truth is that the story of the Mad Gasser will continue to intrigue people and perhaps encourage a few to walk the quiet neighborhoods of Mattoon, contemplating what might have happened during those two weeks in late August and early September 1944. Perhaps some will stop in at the little grocery store on DeWitt Avenue—it's still there—to buy a pack of gum and ponder about Farley Llewellyn and his sisters, and whether they were the culprits. And a few may recall the words of C. S. Lewis, who once wrote: "Child, if you will, it is mythology. It is but truth, not fact: an image, not the very real. But then it is My mythology."

CHAPTER 2

Big Bird on the Loose

Giant flying birdlike monsters have a long history in North America, particularly in Illinois. The state's earliest people had a number of legends about scary, avianlike creatures that often snatched up humans for food. For example, the Potawatomi tribe of Illinois called them *chequah* or *cigwe,* which roughly translates as "thunderbird."

According to Native American lore, the thunderbird was so named because when it flew, the flapping of its colossal wings made a sound like a loud thunderclap and shed drops of rain. When it blinked, it brought lightning. It was always seen flying in front of a storm front, which led many to believe it brought violent weather.

Given the strength of the thunderstorms often experienced in the Midwest, the thunderbird was as good an explanation for bad weather as anything else. The massive birds weren't restricted to Illinois, however. Legends about thunderbirds can be found in Native American cultures from Maine to Alaska and among indigenous peoples in many countries.

According to Mark Hall, author of *Thunderbirds: America's Living Legends of Giant Birds,* the first reported sighting of a thunderbird in Illinois occurred on September 22, 1868, when James Henry of Mound City shot and killed an enormous bird near the town of Cairo.

Hall cited a Cairo *Democrat* newspaper article that noted the bird was bigger than an ostrich and weighed more than one hundred pounds. It was said to have a wingspan of fifteen feet and was spotted while "preying upon a full-sized sheep that it had carried from the ground."

The *Democrat* continued: "This strange species of bird, which is said to have existed extensively during the days of the mastodon, is almost entirely extinct. . . . Its flight across the town and river was witnessed by hundreds of citizens."

More recent reports of thunderbird sightings in Illinois began in the middle part of the twentieth century with a rash of big bird sightings. One of the most credible occurred on April 4, 1948, near Alton, when retired Army Colonel Walter F. Siegmund claimed he saw a huge bird pass above his head.

"It looked too incredible. I thought there was something wrong with my eyesight," he told writer Loren Coleman, author of *Mothman and Other Curious Encounters*, which was published in 2002. "But it was definitely a bird and not a glider or a jet plane."

A few days later on April 9, a farmer named Robert Price saw something similar. Price and his wife, who lived on a farm near the hamlet of Caledonia in northern Illinois, encountered something that he called "a monster bird." He said it was larger than an airplane and had a long neck and giant, powerful wings.

After reports about Price's sighting surfaced, a truck driver named Veryl Babb of Freeport, came forward and said he, too, had seen an extraordinarily large bird that same day but in a different location.

Coleman listed several other Illinois sightings during that time, including in Overland, Richmond Heights, and Alton. The latter involved E. M. Coleman (no relation) and his fifteen-year-old son, James, who saw something big in the air on April 24, 1948.

"It was an enormous, incredible thing with a body that looked like a naval torpedo," E. M. Coleman said. "It was flying at about five hundred feet and cast a shadow the same size as that of a Piper Cub [aircraft] at the same height."

The next significant sighting happened on May 10, 1968, when Grant and Wilma Callison of Galesburg, said they saw three giant bird creatures outside their kitchen window.

According to an account later written by Grant Callison, "I looked out the window and saw a giant 'bird-like' creature . . . I called my wife, Wilma, and we both ran out the back door to get a better look. To our amazement there were three of them."

Callison said the trio of flying creatures were moving at twenty-five to thirty miles per hour and looked "like they had either feathers or scales with a metallic appearance that glowed fluorescent with the light reflected on them. They didn't seem to have a neck, just a head. Their tail was short and seemed to be cone-shaped. The wing spread was approximately 15 to 20 feet. It was really an unbelievable sight, and frightening."

But perhaps the most intriguing modern-day account of a similar encounter occurred in the central Illinois town of Lawndale on July 25, 1977. At about eight o'clock in the evening, ten-year-old Marlon Lowe was playing hide-and-seek in his backyard with friends Travis Goodwin and Michael Thompson.

Terrifying, giant birds have long had a place in Native American lore. This classic photo by Edward S. Curtis, taken circa 1914, shows a masked member of the Qagyuhi tribe impersonating a fierce thunderbird during a marriage ceremony.

Lowe recounted that two extremely large birds suddenly appeared and came at Goodwin, who escaped by diving into a small swimming pool. They then pivoted in the air and swooped down on Lowe.

According to Mark Hall,

> The next thing he knew they were right over him. One bird picked him up by the straps of his sleeveless shirt and lifted him about 2 feet (60 centimeters) off the ground. As the bird carried the boy's 65-pound (30-kilogram) weight, Marlon screamed for his mother and punched at the bird. The bird dropped him to the ground after flying 35 or 40 feet (10.6 or 12 meters) from the backyard to the front yard.

Hall said that Lowe's parents, Ruth and Jake Lowe, as well as two friends, Betty and Jim Daniels, heard the boy's cries and ran into the yard in time to see the bird grasping Marlon in its talons and attempting to fly off with him.

Ruth Lowe later said the bird had an eight- to ten-foot wingspan, a black body that appeared to be more than four feet long, and a white ring around a long neck. She said that after the giant bird dropped her son, it rejoined its companion in the sky and the two creatures flew north into some trees along nearby Kickapoo Creek.

In the book *Creatures of the Outer Edge,* coauthor Jerome Clark interviewed Ruth Lowe within days of the encounter and described her as a down-to-earth, forty-five-year-old grand-mother and local small business owner who had become ridi-culed by many after reporting the event.

"She, in my opinion, is a very honest woman and stated if I didn't believe her she didn't even want to talk about it," Clark noted. "The Logan County Game Warden allegedly sat at her table and called her a liar. All in all, she felt people were laughing at her for what she had seen."

Despite such skepticism a United Press International (UPI) story that appeared in newspapers throughout the country a few days after the attack played the story fairly straightforward, quot-ing Ruth Lowe and James Daniels about what they had seen, and noting, "Logan County officials said the story was not being discounted because of the number of credible witnesses who reported seeing the birds."

The article, however, also noted that "experts" knew of no indigenous birds large enough to lift a child and quoted a Logan County conservation officer who said the birds were most likely turkeys or king vultures. Daniels told UPI that he thought they most resembled the rare and endangered California condor, a bird species never seen before in Illinois.

There were additional sightings in central Illinois in the days after the Lawndale incident, including in Armington, Lin-coln, and Shelbyville.

For instance on July 30, "Texas John" Huffer of Tuscola said he, too, had seen the big birds—and even shot some film of them. Huffer, an outdoor writer and photographer, was fishing on Lake Shelbyville when he spotted two enormous black birds perched in a tree.

He said he sounded his boat horn, which caused them to fly off. Huffer, who had been a combat photographer, grabbed his camera and shot about one hundred feet of color film of one of the two birds. He later estimated that bird had a wingspan of about twelve feet.

In a UPI story that appeared on August 1, 1977, Huffer said the birds "made an awful, kind of clacking noise." He described their cry as "primeval." Additionally, Huffer said the two birds left behind other evidence: "droppings the size of base-balls around a dead tree where they apparently roosted."

The Huffer film footage has appeared on a number of television shows, including the *Animal X: Natural Mystery Unit* program, broadcast on the Animal Planet network in 2004.

The last reported sighting of the big birds in the Land of Lincoln during this period occurred on August 11, 1977, when John and Wanda Chappell of Odin, (about sixty miles south of Shelbyville Lake) said they spotted some type of enormous gray-black bird circling over the pond on their farm. The creature landed in a tree about four hundred feet from their house.

"It was so big it had a hard time finding a limb big enough to land on," John Chappell said in a UPI story. Apparently the winged wonder stayed in the tree for five to ten minutes, during which time John and his wife, Wanda, viewed it with binoculars.

Wanda Chappell said it appeared to have a wingspan of about fourteen feet.

"It looked like a prehistoric bird. It was really fantastic," she said in the story. "The head didn't have any feathers and it had a long neck, crooked, kind of 'S' shaped. The body was covered with feathers and was gray or charcoal-colored."

Despite the multiple sightings, many experts remained skeptical about the big birds. They pointed to the fact that no bones or remains of such a creature were (or ever have been) found, and they questioned whether a bird that big could even fly and/or be strong enough to lift a child.

According to Mark Hall, many of the 1977 press accounts quoted ornithologists and wildlife officials—none of whom actually saw the big birds—dismissing the encounters. At least two county conservation officials flatly stated that Marlon Lowe could not have been picked up by any kind of bird, no matter how large it might be, and implied that anyone who said otherwise was mistaken or lying.

William Beecher, an ornithologist and former director of the Chicago Academy of Sciences, noted in Hall's book: "In the whole history of the world there never has been a bird capable of carrying a 65-pound load." Beecher said the reports were simply "hysteria" and people were most likely seeing turkey vultures.

Since then, while sightings of thunderbirds in Illinois have trailed off in the mainstream media, the subject has remained a lively online topic. For example, in a blog titled *Sign of the Times,* an anonymous blogger noted in June 2012: "I saw the two thunderbirds in Springfield, IL the day before Marlon Lowe was attacked in Lawndale, IL. This is no joke! I told my father and family and they all laughed. But in the next day or two when it hit the local news they changed their tune!"

Another blog, *Biofort*, maintained by Scott Maruna, a Jacksonville high school chemistry and physics teacher and author of *The Mad Gasser of Mattoon*, included the account of an Illinois man named Tom Sheets who claimed that on October 26, 2008, at about 1:15 p.m., he had seen two giant birds south of Lacon.

Sheets, described as an avid outdoorsman and longtime land surveyor, said he was sitting in his truck in his driveway, waiting for traffic to clear, when he spotted the big birds. "These birds had a wing span of at least 10 feet," he told Maruna. "They were at least five times larger than a hawk."

Sheets said the birds resembled a turkey vulture, with which he was familiar, except they were wider in the shoulders and had different markings. He said he later looked in his birding guidebook and thought they actually looked more like California condors.

Interestingly, Illinois is also home to another mythical creature often lumped in with the thunderbird legends. According to many sources a terrible birdlike monster known as the "Piasá" once existed in the southwestern portion of the state near present-day St. Louis.

The first written account of the Piasá was in the diaries of explorers Louis Jolliet and Jacques Marquette, who, during their

1673 expedition on the Mississippi River, came upon cliffs north of present-day Alton, Illinois, that were painted with a mysterious giant mural depicting a ferocious horned animal. Marquette described it as being as large as a calf, with antlers on its head, terrible red eyes, a long fish tail, a bearded face like a man, and scales covering its body. While Marquette copied the image in his notes, unfortunately all of his papers were lost during his return trip. Interestingly, the image described by Marquette did not have wings.

A later drawing by French mapmaker Jean-Baptiste-Louis Franquelin, based on Marquette's description, depicted a weasel-like animal with long thin claws, a human head, fish scales, deer antlers, and a tail ending in fish fins that stretched around its body . . . but no wings.

However, according to Mark Hall, "Later travelers who came along, up to the year 1699, differed with Marquette, apparently because the appearance of the pictographs changed with the relative wetness and dryness of the seasons. They saw that the Piasá also had wings."

In a 1956 article that appeared in the *Journal of the Illinois State Historical Society* titled, "The Piasá Bird: Fact or Fiction?" Dr. Wayne C. Temple noted that travelers ceased mentioning seeing the mural on the cliff after the late 1690s, when it appeared it had been obliterated by weathering.

However, in 1836 John Russell, a professor at the nearby Alton Seminary, published an essay, "The Piasá: An Indian

Tradition of Illinois," which resurrected the legend of the Piasá—but with some significant enhancements. In it Russell offered a meaning for the word *Piasá*, claiming it was an Illini Indian word meaning "the bird that devours men." He also said the mural on the bluff outside of Alton is an artistic representation of this terrible bird monster and offered a somewhat romanticized explanation of the legend surrounding the bird.

According to Russell, "many thousand moons before the arrival of the pale faces," there existed a bird creature so large it could carry off a full-grown deer. "Having obtained a taste of human flesh, from that time he would prey upon nothing else," Russell wrote. "He was artful as he was powerful; would dart suddenly and unexpectedly upon an Indian, bear him off into one of the caves in the bluff, and devour him."

One day a great chief named Ouatogá decided to end the Piasá's reign of terror. A plan of attack came to him in a dream: He would use himself as bait by drawing the attention of the ferocious bird, and then he would have twenty of his best warriors fire arrows at the monster as it swooped in to take him. The scheme worked, and the bird was killed.

"In memory of this event, the image of the Piasá was engraved on the face of the bluff," Russell wrote. "The figure of a large bird cut into the solid rock, is still there, and at a height that is perfectly inaccessible . . . even at this day, an Indian never passes that spot in his canoe without firing his gun at the figure of the bird. The marks of [musket] balls on the rock are almost innumerable."

Russell added that he visited the cave once frequented by the giant bird. After digging down a few feet into the surface, he encountered literally thousands of human bones.

"How, and by whom, and for what purpose [they are there], it is impossible even to conjecture," he concluded.

According to Temple, Russell's fable—which even Russell's son later admitted was never intended to be taken as historical fact—grew in stature over time. Temple said that it was doubtful the mural was visible after about 1698, yet throughout the nineteenth century a number of writers referred to the painting as if it still existed. Most described it as depicting an enormous winged creature.

In 1924 Herbert Forcade, an eighteen-year-old Boy Scout, decided to give new life to the legend of the Piasá. Working with members of his troop, he painted a giant representation of the monster on a cliff north of Alton (the bluff that was the site of the original mural is believed to have been destroyed in the nineteenth century when the area was quarried), this time incorporating the wings first mentioned by Russell.

Since then several different versions of the fantastic monster have been reproduced on the limestone walls overlooking the Mississippi River, including the current image, which was painted in 2000 on a cliff about a mile north of Alton. The image was partially based on the nineteenth-century descriptions of the creature (meaning it, too, includes wings).

Perhaps it's best to give the final word on the Piasá controversy to Temple: "There is little doubt that there were, at one time, painted figures on the bluff at Alton, but Marquette's sketch of them is lost," he wrote. "Not until John Russell published his tale of the Piasá Bird in 1836 was there any account of wings on the figure."

But what about the stories of Illinois's truly winged thunderbirds, which are clearly not the product of a nineteenth-century scholar's overactive imagination? Those who have seen or encountered the freakishly large fowl in recent decades believe they've seen something extraordinary.

While these birds didn't create thunder with their wings or flash lightning out of their eyes, they were larger than any known bird species and—at least according to the Lowe family—capable of carrying a child for a short time.

Why, then, is there no proof of their existence? Hall believes the reason is because we've never tried to seriously look for the birds in order to protect them.

"Mankind takes a largely selfish attitude toward its fellow animals. Birds are treated as food or put into service," he wrote. "Thunderbirds, if they exist, do not serve mankind and, while not necessarily benign, are not a major nuisance."

CHAPTER 3

Macomb's Firebug

The first strange fire at the Willey home appeared on August 7, 1948. Mrs. Charles (Lou, also called Lulu) Willey, sixty-three, spotted smoke coming from behind the wood-fired kitchen stove. She put out the flames and surmised that sparks from the stove probably ignited the fire. It was peculiar but perhaps not unexpected in an old farmhouse.

However, a few hours later she watched with confusion as a brown spot suddenly appeared on the wallpaper near the kitchen ceiling and then burst into flames. She quickly beat out the small blaze and began to wonder: What in the world is happening to my house?

* * *

Lou and her husband, Charles Willey, sixty-eight, had lived for more than twenty-six years in their comfortable wooden two-story farmhouse in Bethel Township, located about twelve miles south of the western Illinois community of Macomb.

Charles was the great grandson of Absalom Willey, a pioneer settler in McDonough County—in fact Charles Willey's grandfather, also named Charles, had built the farmhouse and many of its barns and other farm buildings.

In the summer of 1948, Arthur McNeil Sr., who was Lou Willey's brother, and his two children, twelve-year-old Wonet and nine-year-old Arthur Jr., moved in with the Willeys. The senior McNeil, who was raising the children following a divorce five years earlier, had been hired to work in a local factory.

While Arthur Jr. seemed happy with his new home, the red-haired, bespectacled Wonet was not. She had wanted to live with her remarried mother, Mrs. Leona Eagle, who resided in Bloomington. Although she kept her resentment to herself—her father later said she never asked to go live with her mother—she missed her mother and dreaded moving into a remote farmhouse miles from any town.

* * *

On August 11 the Willey farmhouse experienced a rash of unexplained fires. According to eyewitness accounts, new brown spots appeared on wallpaper throughout the house. As the spots would flare up and begin to burn, the Willeys, aided by neighbors Walter Stoneking and his wife, doused them with cups of water.

After a restless night the Willeys spent the following day tearing the wallpaper off the walls—assuming that it was somehow the cause of the strange fiery outbreaks. But the fires continued, with the wooden lathes in the plaster suddenly bursting into flames.

Not wanting to lose all of their possessions, the Willeys removed most of the furniture and other valuables from the house. The family also decided to sleep in the garage.

Walter Stoneking noted in a later newspaper story that while he was removing items from the house, he draped a lace curtain across the foot of a brass headboard in one of the upstairs bedrooms. When he returned, he found the curtain turned to ash.

On August 13 the farmhouse was engulfed in flames. "A series of fires which have beset the Charles Willey family, Macomb route four, since last Saturday ended this morning when the house burned to the ground," reported the *Macomb Daily Journal* that day. "Cause of the blazes is a mystery to the Willeys."

It was a mystery to everyone else as well. The *Macomb Daily Journal* story noted that the Willey farmhouse had no electrical wiring and that many of the fires broke out in parts of the house well away from the stove. "Neither the Willeys nor their neighbors can even suggest an explanation," reported the paper. "The Willeys do not suspect arson."

The mysterious burning of the Willey farmhouse sparked intense local interest. The *Macomb Daily Journal* began to publish nearly daily updates on the fires' investigation.

On August 16, under the headline, "Willeys Still Baffled By Series Of Blazes," the paper quoted Lou Willey saying that in the days leading up to the inferno that finally destroyed the farmhouse she had seen "more than a hundred, yes, two hundred fires" breaking out in the house.

"I'm not superstitious, don't believe in ghosts or anything like that, but there sure is something wrong about that place," she said. "I don't know what it is but it's not scaring us. We will build again and right on the same foundation."

Disaster struck again on August 17. The Willeys' dairy barn burned down—again for no apparent reason.

This abandoned farmhouse south of Macomb sits near the site of the former Willey Farm.

"The barn fire is as much a mystery as the series of blazes that broke out in the farm house," reported the *Journal*. "The barn which is located several hundred feet from the house caught fire about 15 minutes after the Willeys had been to it to do their milking. As far as they know no other person had been near the barn all day. No one smoked in or near the barn during the milking."

The newspaper also noted, "There is no suspicion on the part of Willey or neighbors that any of the fires were deliberately set."

A day later the *Macomb Daily Journal* reported that the Willeys and McNeils were now living in a makeshift tent on the farm. The paper speculated that fly spray or the wallpaper paste might have been the culprit for the fires. It said the Willeys frequently used an insecticide in and around their house and barn buildings.

The paper quoted Dr. C. W. Bennett of the chemistry department at Western Illinois Teachers College in Macomb (now Western Illinois University) as saying that fly sprays use white phosphorus, which could have resulted in the spontaneous blazes.

However, Dr. Bennett added, he had never heard of fly spray causing such fires and thought it was "improbable." Additionally, neighbors used the same brand of spray and none of them had experienced any spontaneous fires.

By this time the rash of bizarre fires on the Willey farm had attracted the attention of statewide and national media. Soon

Macomb was awash with reporters from newspapers from as far away as Chicago.

"100 Fires Get Best of House," said the headline of an August 18 story appearing in the *Chicago Tribune*. The paper said not only local officials but also the state fire marshal's office were investigating the outbreak of fires.

"The persistently reoccurring flames stirred nonplussed residents to half joking, half fearsome comments of supernatural forces and antics as bizarre as comic strip oddities," noted the *Tribune*.

"Nobody ever heard of anything like it," John Burgard, a state deputy fire marshal, told the United Press wire service on August 18. "I saw it with my own eyes. A little brown spot, and first thing you know a fire would break out. Everybody thought there were ghosts around there."

Despite the presence of investigators and reporters, more phantom fires—as some newspapers were calling them—broke out on the Willey farm the next day. This time the Willeys' chicken coop and milk house caught on fire.

Fortunately both fires were quickly extinguished, but investigators remained perplexed as to the cause. No one had seen anyone near the two buildings prior to the flare-ups and neither of the structures had been sprayed with insecticides or contained any wallpaper paste.

On August 20, yet another barn on the farm burned to the ground. At about five o'clock in the evening, a barn containing hay and straw suddenly ignited. In less than twenty minutes, the entire barn was destroyed.

The *Journal* reported:

> Arthur McNeil Jr., 9, a nephew who lives with the Willeys, was the first to see the smoke yesterday evening. He was pumping water for the calves and his sister, Juanette [her name was spelled as Juanette, Wanet, and Wonet in various newspapers], 12, was collecting eggs from the barn.
>
> Arthur said he heard a "crackle like something burning" when he was in the barn playing with the calves a few minutes earlier. He said he left the calves in the barn when his uncle told him to pump the water. While he was at the well in front of the barn his sister came out with the eggs. "It was about two minutes after she left the barn that I saw the smoke," he said. "I yelled that the barn was burning."

Fortunately the fire was in the upper loft and the boy was able to open the barn doors to allow the calves to escape. A sidebar story quoted a technician from Wright Field, a US Army Air Corps base near Riverside, Ohio, who suggested that the Willey fires might have been caused by haywire radio frequencies being tested at the field.

Louis C. Gust, described as a radio expert at Wright Field, said the base was testing the remote ignition of materials using radio waves. "Suppose you had some material test that could be ignited by radio and you wanted to test it for possible sabotage value," Gust told the paper. "Would you pick a city? No, you'd pick some out-of-the-way place, like the Willey farm."

The fires began to take a toll on the Willeys, who accepted an offer from neighbor Jim Thompson to live in a vacant farmhouse on his property.

"It's an awful thing to see such queer fires, to have your house burn down, then one barn, then another barn," Lou Willey told Irene Burner of the *Macomb Daily Journal*. "I just don't understand it. I wish we knew what was causing all these fires."

In the same story Burner melodramatically concluded: "The scene of what two weeks ago was an ordinary farm is a picture of devastation now. Ashes and rubbish are all that remain of the house and two barns."

Not surprisingly in the days following the burning of the second barn, the Willey farm became the object of considerable public interest. Media accounts said that hundreds of people began showing up at the site hoping to see if something—anything—else was going to burn up.

"The latest development increased the number of reporters, photographers and sight-seers who have swarmed to the Willey farm since the mysterious character of the phantom fires first attracted nation-wide attention," the August 21 *Journal* said. "The Willeys were tired of questions and conversation. They were tired of visitors. They were near exhaustion."

Meanwhile the investigation continued. Dr. A. G. Singh, formerly at the University of Illinois and an expert on volatile fuels and chemicals, was invited by the state fire marshal's office to study the site and offer his conclusions.

After visiting the site, he told the media he had nothing to report but would continue his investigation. Professor John J. Ahern, director of safety engineering at the Illinois Institute of Technology, surveyed the damage and told the *Chicago Tribune* that it was his opinion that the house fires were the result of a buildup of combustible gases in the walls that ignited when they came in contact with the air.

He said the barn fires appeared to be the result of carelessness or were intentionally set and dismissed talk of either supernatural origins or random radio waves.

Two days later Macomb Fire Chief Fred Wilson stunned everyone by announcing that he believed the fires were the work of an arsonist using a box of "plain old matches." Wilson said the presence of so many people in the area had discouraged the firebug from setting any additional fires.

"There weren't no fires on Sunday," he said. "And I don't think there will be as long as people are around, if you know what I mean."

On August 28 a small fire mysteriously broke out in a kitchen cupboard in the Thompson house, where the Willeys and McNeils had relocated.

Lou Willey said that at about one o'clock in the afternoon she was canning tomatoes in the kitchen and smelled smoke. She found a newspaper on a cupboard shelf was on fire and threw water on it before it could spread. She said she was the only person in the house at the time; the two McNeil children were outside playing in the yard.

Two days later, on August 30, authorities announced they had solved the mystery of the phantom fires.

"Set Fires, Wanted To Go Live With Mother, Girl, 13, Confesses," said the headline at the top of page two in the *Macomb Daily Journal*. According to the accompanying story, Wonet McNeil, who would turn thirteen the next day, admitted she had set all of the fires at the Willey and Thompson farms.

"The girl believed that if she burned the Willey buildings, she would be sent to live with her mother," the paper said.

Lou Willey was quoted as saying that the girl must have been "awful slick" in being able to set the fires without anyone seeing her. She described Wonet as an obedient and well-behaved child who seemed to be happy living at the Willey home.

According to the story, Deputy State Fire Marshal John Burgard "trapped" Wonet into confessing. After interviewing all of the other family members, he dismissed them to do their chores and left Wonet alone for several minutes in the Thompson house.

He also set a box of matches in a wall box at a certain angle. After he returned, he smelled smoke in the house. He started to look for it and Wonet helpfully pointed to the kitchen ceiling and said, "There it is." He said he thought there might be another fire and again she helped him by pointing out a small fire in a bedroom wall.

After checking the wall box and noticing the matches had been disturbed, he decided to spring his trap. He told her she had been the only person in the house and all of the evidence pointed to her as the arsonist.

Wonet first denied the charge and was backed by Mrs. Willey, who had returned to the house. When Burgard pressed her, she began to cry and refused to answer any more questions.

Later that day Burgard and State's Attorney Keith Scott interrogated Wonet, but she continued to deny the accusations.

The next morning, after being told by her father to tell the truth, Wonet was taken to Macomb for further questioning by Burgard and Scott.

"It's time you started to tell the truth," the paper quoted Burgard as saying to Wonet. After again denying any involvement, Wonet finally cracked and admitted she had set all of the fires.

In a partial transcript of the interview, which appeared in the *Journal*, Wonet appeared alternately defiant, confused, and contrite as she reluctantly revealed details of how she started the fires.

"Why did you tell me Saturday you wouldn't tell me any more and start to cry? What were you afraid of?" asked Burgard at one point.

"I wasn't afraid of nothing," shot back Wonet.

Later in the interview Wonet acknowledged starting three of the fires. Burgard responded by telling her they were going to take her to a special hospital in Chicago for intelligence tests.

"They are going to ask you some questions to determine if you are as intelligent as a normal girl of your age, but if you are still holding back something in the state attorney's office, which I think you are, you won't be able to answer those questions and they will say now that girl has got something the matter with her and maybe she has got something the matter that makes her start three fires," Burgard said. "Tell Mr. Scott about the fires."

To this Wonet simply said, "What ones? I set them all."

The girl said she had pried loose wallpaper to set some of the fires, ignited newspapers and straw to begin others, and climbed on chairs to set the fires in higher locations. She said she had done it all using matches from the kitchen.

Despite her confession, some still questioned how she set all of blazes.

"No one was able to fully explain today how Wonet, using no more than a match, could have ignited the walls in a manner that mystified members of the family and all of the neighbors," noted the *Journal*.

At a later press conference, State's Attorney Scott said he was not going to prosecute Wonet for setting the fires. "The state's only interest is in helping her reconstruct her life," he said.

An August 31 story in the *Journal* sought to give some perspective to the whole affair. In the article Dr. Sophie Schroeder Sloman, a Chicago psychiatrist who interviewed Wonet, said the girl was the "victim of a family mixup and divorce . . . a nice little kid caught in the middle."

That same day the *Bloomington Pantagraph* contained a short article saying Wonet's mother, Mrs. Leona Eagle, did not believe her daughter had set the fires. The paper also quoted Eagle's sister, Mrs. Opal Simpkins, who said: "We don't think she did it. Wonet couldn't have been that clever and that fast. She is not stupid but she couldn't have acted as quickly as they say."

On September 24, following a brief hearing, Wonet was ordered by a McDonough County Court to live with her grandmother, Mrs. John (Daisy) Johnson of Marseilles, Illinois. The girl had been temporarily placed in her grandmother's custody following her confession, and the court—supported by the state's attorney's office and her father—decided to make the arrangement permanent.

After the court hearing Wonet McNeil disappeared from the pages of local and state newspapers. The last mention of the girl was in an October 30, 1998, article in the *Macomb Journal* that recapped the entire affair but ended on a cryptic note: "Wonet McNeil died in 1948 and took with her the secrets of the Willey fires."

Today it's difficult to find the site of the old Willey farm. Most of the farmhouses that once dotted that part of southern McDonough County—known as Gin Ridge—are gone. You can still find the old Willey family cemetery, where Charles Willey's great-grandfather, grandfather, and father are buried (Charles was laid to rest in Macomb).

In recent decades a coal strip-mining company has reshaped much of the surrounding landscape. Yet despite the changes brought by the passage of time, it's still possible to imagine how a young Wonet McNeil might have felt after arriving there in the summer of 1948.

She would look at the deep hollows and rolling hills, the ribbons of forest and fields of farmland, and perhaps think she had arrived in the most desolate place in the world. Loaded down with all of the chores that come with farm life, and with only a little brother for companionship, she might grow bored. And look for things to fight the boredom.

Maybe even play with matches.

CHAPTER 4

Tragedy in the Suburbs

Few crimes have gained as much attention as the unsolved murder of Valerie Jeanne Percy, the twenty-one-year-old daughter of former US Senator Charles Percy of Illinois. Early on the morning of September 18, 1966, an unknown assailant broke into Percy's elegant home on the banks of Lake Michigan, then bludgeoned and stabbed the young woman to death.

PERCY'S DAUGHTER SLAIN! screamed a large front-page headline in the *Chicago Tribune* on the afternoon of the murder—the first of hundreds that would appear in newspapers throughout the country.

The shocking and brutal murder was big news. Charles Percy, former president of the Chicago-based Bell & Howell Corporation, a major national manufacturer of camera equipment, was a rising star in the state's Republican Party. In September 1966 he had narrowly lost a race for governor and was locked in a tightly contested race against Illinois's incumbent US Senator Paul Douglas, a Democrat.

Charles Percy seemed to have it all. He'd achieved remarkable business success, earning his first million while in his early thirties. He was young (only forty-seven), athletic (an avid tennis player), and handsome in a preppy way. He had a beautiful wife and five attractive children. Some suggested that if he beat Douglas, he might even be in line for the presidency.

Among those working on Percy's senate campaign was Valerie, recently graduated from Cornell University, who was described in a *Chicago Tribune* story as "intelligent," "gracious," and "vivacious." An attractive young woman with blonde hair and blue eyes, Valerie was in charge of working with campaign volunteers.

"She plunged into her father's campaign, interviewing and recruiting volunteers and spending long hours placing them in more than 20 neighborhood centers in the Chicago area," the *Tribune* noted.

The paper quoted a coworker who said, "Val always took the subway so she wouldn't tie up the family cars. She was that kind of person, very thoughtful."

In another story, which included interviews with her college friends, Valerie was called "well-adjusted and well-liked" by a Cornell administrator and "one of the most charming girls I had in class . . . the most disarmingly gentle person I've ever known," by Professor J. J. Demorest, chairman of Cornell's French literature department and her school adviser.

Valerie's brutal murder deeply shocked her friends, coworkers, and family. Two days after the attack, one psychiatrist told the *Tribune* that, based on the evidence, Valerie "died at the hands of a person in a fit of rage." According to Dr. Edward J. Kelleher, a psychiatrist for the Municipal Court of Chicago, the motive may have been vengeance or jealousy, and the act most likely was performed by an emotionally disturbed person.

Another physician, Dr. Robert Hohf, a neighbor of the Percy family who arrived at the house within minutes of the attack and pronounced Valerie dead, said the violent nature of the killing showed it was the work of "a madman."

Hohf told the *Tribune,* "Anybody doing that kind of violence is doing it for some sort of abnormal drive and I am convinced there is some sexual motivation behind it . . . this atrocity was committed by some deranged person."

So what happened in the three-story, seventeen-room Percy home at 40 Devonshire Lane in the posh North Chicago suburb of Kenilworth on the morning of September 18, 1966, just before five o'clock in the morning?

In numerous interviews and accounts, family members and friends reconstructed the events of the night before. Valerie had eaten dinner at home with her fraternal twin sister Sharon, thirteen-year-old sister Gail, eleven-year-old brother Mark, mother Loraine, and two campaign staff members, James Mann and Tully Friedman.

At about ten o'clock Mann and Friedman departed for the evening and Valerie excused herself to go to bed. At about forty, her sister Sharon returned from a date and stopped by Valerie's room to return a raincoat she had borrowed.

According to Sharon's later testimony, Valerie was sitting in bed watching television when she bid her goodnight. Sharon recalled that she tossed the coat on the bed and her sister said, "Sharon, don't lay it there. It will get wrinkled." She hung the coat in a closet and headed to her room to retire.

At about twelve thirty in the morning Charles Percy returned home from a campaign speech in downtown Chicago and looked in on Valerie. He later told police that she was asleep with the lights out and the television turned off.

He went to his room, located down the hall from Valerie's room, where he joined his wife in watching television until about one thirty, at which point both of them retired for the evening.

Sometime before five in the morning, an unknown person broke into the Percy residence. The intruder cut a hole in a screen and then apparently used a glasscutter to make an opening in a glass panel in the French door (there was also some evidence that the person might have taped the glass and shattered it to make the opening large enough for his or her hand). The person unlatched the door and entered the house.

Investigators initially believed the person might have been someone known to the Percy family, because the Percy's Labrador retriever did not bark. The police also concluded that the person was familiar with the layout of the house, because he seemed to know where he was going once inside the large house.

He crept through the music room and passed through a large living room before coming to a vestibule. From there he climbed the eighteen steps of a circular stairway before reaching the second floor.

On this floor he would have had to pass Sharon's bedroom and the unoccupied bedroom of Mark, who was on an overnight camping trip with friends, before reaching Valerie's bedroom, which was located at the northeast corner of the house.

Charles and Loraine's master bedroom and Gail's bedroom were located at the other end of the hallway, about thirty-five feet away from Valerie's room.

"The attacker obviously came into the house to murder someone," Dr. Andrew J. Toman, Cook County coroner, told the *Tribune* shortly after the attack.

At an inquest a few weeks after the murder, Loraine testified that she had been awakened before five o'clock by the sound of broken glass—she thought one of her children might have dropped a glass filled with water—and movement on the first floor.

"I heard a noise, I don't know exactly what it was. Then the steps. I don't know how late after that that I heard a low moan from one of the girl's bedrooms like someone was sick," she said. "I was half asleep. And then I don't know how long but I heard another moan and I got up and walked down the hall calling out Valerie's name . . . I saw a light coming from under the door of her bedroom."

Loraine said she opened the door and froze. A man with a flashlight was leaning over Valerie's bed. She told police that he appeared to be about five feet, eight inches tall and about 160 pounds.

"I saw he had on a light or white shirt or jacket and it was checkered, wide checks," she said. "The shirt or jacket did not go to his wrists because I saw his forearms. His trousers and belt were a dark color. Then he turned and shone the light in my face and I noticed a dark outline and the shape of his head and hairline."

At this point, Loraine said, she began to scream for her husband and ran back to her bedroom. She triggered a home security system, setting off a loud siren on the roof of the house.

The commotion awakened Charles, who testified that he grabbed the telephone and called the operator to report an emergency at the house. He ran to Valerie's room.

"There she was lying in bed," he said at the inquest. "I remember distinctly seeing her right side covered with blood."

In the meantime the attacker had disappeared from Valerie's room. While Loraine rushed back to her daughter's side (she said she thought she felt a pulse and tried to comfort her daughter), Charles believed the intruder had gone downstairs, so he raced to the first floor, hoping to catch him at the front door, but found it was still locked and chained (he didn't realize the man entered from a different door).

Charles immediately thought of the case of notorious serial killer Richard Speck, who a few months earlier had raped and murdered eight nurses in Chicago, and ran back upstairs where he thought the man might still be hiding. He gathered together his family and they searched the house, finding no one.

Charles also called his neighbor, Dr. Hohf, asking him to come over to help Valerie. Hohf arrived within a few minutes but found the girl was already dead.

Hohf told newspapers that the young woman's neck and head were covered with "numerous and very disfiguring stab wounds" that indicated the killer might have been acting out a deep hatred for her.

The coroner said that it appeared that Valerie had tried to protect herself as she was attacked. He said her legs were drawn up and her arms were thrown over her face. And while there was no evidence of a sexual attack, Valerie's nightgown was pulled up to near her ribs.

Police said that based on the wounds, the attacker used a weapon with a triangular head, such as a fireplace poker or a ball-peen hammer, to batter Valerie about the head and then stabbed her repeatedly with a large double-edged knife. The coroner said Valerie was killed by four blows to the head, shattering her skull. Additionally, she had been stabbed fourteen times.

Because of the high-profile nature of the crime, the Chicago Police Department quickly agreed to assist the small, fourteen-member Kenilworth Police Department, which had never dealt with a murder investigation.

Soon, scuba divers were scouring the bottom of nearby Lake Michigan, while experienced detectives and forensic experts were examining the home and surrounding grounds.

On September 23 the *Tribune* reported that the divers had pulled up a bayonet that could have been used to stab Valerie. Additionally, about a dozen fingerprints and palm prints had been pulled from the Percy home.

As the investigation plodded forward, additional details trickled out. The police ruled out robbery as a motive since Valerie's wallet and purse were untouched and nothing was missing from the house.

There were footprints on the sandy beach area outside of the house, but no sand was found inside the house. Outside of the house police had found a pair of scissors, a pocketknife, and a worn brown shoe, but all were tested and found to have no connection with the crime. The Percy family offered a $50,000 reward for the murderer's capture.

On September 19 Charles Percy temporarily suspended his campaign for the Senate—as did his opponent Senator Paul Douglas—and two days later the family took off for an undisclosed location in California to grieve.

Throughout the entire ordeal the family made few public comments, preferring to keep their pain private. In his 1968 book *Charles Percy of Illinois,* author David Murray wrote that during the days immediately following the murder "the family sat, shrunken in aspect, drawn into themselves, with shock serving as a kind of armor plate for emotion."

Three weeks later Charles Percy announced that, after discussing the matter with his family, he was resuming his campaign.

"As the Bible says, there is a time for every purpose under the sun—a time to be born, a time to die; a time to mourn, a time to dance," Percy said somberly. "With so little time remaining, I think it is time to speak."

He defeated Douglas in November and served in the Senate until 1985.

Meanwhile police continued to follow up on leads. One of those was an anonymous phone call stating that a man had been seen sitting in a car outside of the Percy house, looking at it, at about one o'clock that morning. Nothing, however, came of the tip.

Another was the confession, in early October, of an eighteen-year-old vagrant in Arizona. A few days later the youth recanted the confession and noted the only reason he claimed responsibility was that he wanted to die.

In mid-October an emotionally disturbed nineteen-year-old Oak Lawn man confessed to the Percy killing—as well as a number of crimes that never happened—so police eliminated him as a suspect.

Still later, police tried to find a "barefoot man," who reportedly was seen walking on the beach only a short time after the murder. The man, who was never found, was described as wearing a white T-shirt and khaki pants. Eventually more than a dozen different people would step forward to "confess" to committing the crime.

By December Kenilworth police chief Robert P. Daley said investigators had questioned more than twenty-five hundred people in twenty-five states and several other countries and given lie detector tests to fourteen of them but still had no solid leads.

Shortly after his election Senator-elect Percy sold the house in which his daughter had been slain to neighbors and longtime friends, William and Edna Graham. Percy said his wife was afraid to stay in it.

In 2008 the Graham estate (William died in 2006 and Edna in 1981) sold the home, which was demolished in 2010 so a newer, larger mansion could be erected on the 2.5-acre site.

As time passed, the story began to fade from public awareness. But in 1970 a fugitive Chicago man arrested for a rape and robbery case that had occurred in Pennsylvania three years earlier told police that his partner in the crime, Frederick J. Malchow, had confessed that he (Malchow) had killed Valerie Percy when she caught him burglarizing the house.

Harold James Evans said that while sharing a jail cell, Malchow told him he had stabbed and beaten Valerie Percy to death. According to the *Tribune,* Evans submitted to a polygraph test, which indicated he was telling the truth.

Unfortunately Malchow, who was also from Chicago, could not be questioned about his possible involvement in the murder. In 1967, shortly after Evans and Malchow were convicted of the Pennsylvania rape and robbery, the two men escaped as they were being led from the courthouse to the county jail. Malchow's body was discovered two days later in shallow water beneath a railroad bridge near Norristown, Pennsylvania. Investigators said he had fallen and died.

Police initially did not give much credence to Evans's story, but in 1973 the *Chicago Sun Times* published a series of stories, which won a 1974 Pulitzer Prize, claiming Malchow may have been involved in the murder.

According to the stories, Malchow and Evans were part of a four-man gang of mob-backed burglars who had been hitting Chicago's wealthy suburbs. The *Sun Times* said that a dying gangster, Leo Rugendorf, told the paper's reporters he had something he wanted to get off his chest before he died and pointed them to another member of the gang, Francis "Frank" Hohimer.

"They'll get me for the Valerie Percy murder," Rugendorf said Hohimer had told him. "The girl woke up, and I hit her on the head with a pistol."

Hohimer's own brother, Harold "Wayne" Hohimer, corroborated Rugendorf's claim, telling the *Sun Times* that his brother had admitted he had to "off a girl" during a robbery attempt.

Wayne Hohimer said that his brother had told him he killed a young woman because she "made a lot of noise and they got in a fight . . . He was talking about the Valerie Percy thing."

Yet another person told the *Sun Times* that, two weeks before the Valerie Percy murder, Frank Hohimer had talked about how he was "casing" the Percy house in order to rob it.

However, Frank Hohimer, who was serving a fifteen- to thirty-year sentence in prison, denied any involvement in the murder and blamed it on the deceased Fred Malchow. He said Malchow had appeared at his doorstep on the morning of the murder, wearing bloody clothing and asking for a change of clothes as well as a place to stash his car. Frank Hohimer said he gave Malchow new clothing before burning the bloody garments in his apartment incinerator and torching the car.

Perhaps adding more credibility to the story that someone from the gang was involved in the killing was the revelation by investigators that a two-minute telephone call had been made on May 2, 1966, (more than four months before the murder) from the Percy home to a Southern Chicago grocery store owned by Rugendorf, who acknowledged he often helped plan the gang's robberies and "fenced" their stolen goods.

In the end, however, authorities did not have sufficient evidence to charge either Frank Hohimer or Fred Malchow with the crime.

Over the past few decades, Valerie Percy's murder has been the subject of countless online crime forums, cable crime shows, and mystery books, as well as the occasional newspaper or TV story. In September 2011 there was a flurry of new stories about the crime following the death of Charles Percy at the age of ninety-one.

The family has a long-standing offer of a $100,000 reward to anyone who might have information that would solve the crime. To date no one has ever been arrested for the murder.

In 1966, the 21-year-old daughter of former US Senator Charles Percy of Illinois (shown here) was brutally murdered in the family home near Chicago.

CHAPTER 5

Burning Mysteries

No one quite understands exactly how it happened. The only potential witness died. But on Christmas Eve in 1885, seventy-two-year-old Matilda Rooney of the north-central Illinois town of Seneca suddenly and unexpectedly burst into flames and was almost instantly incinerated.

The event is one of the earliest known documented accounts of the paranormal phenomenon known as spontaneous human combustion (SHC). Essentially, SHC occurs when, for no apparent reason, a human body abruptly catches on fire and burns to ashes at an extremely high temperature. Bizarrely, the fire usually only incinerates the person and does not spread throughout the room.

According to author Nelson Acquilano, who has studied the phenomenon, there have been more than two hundred reports of individuals mysteriously erupting in flames and burning to death over the past three centuries.

Acquilano noted that there are several theories for how SHC might occur, including a buildup of certain intestinal gases that may be flammable when exposed to air, such as phosphorous, or the presence of chemicals or fats in the body that are normally harmless but that become more explosive when combined in a certain way or triggered by something, such as alcohol saturation (many of the cases involve heavy drinkers or alcoholics) and possibly cigarette smoke.

"Testing and evidence, however, disproves these theories for human combustion," Acquilano added. "In many cases they may cause a fire, but burn at too low a temperature for the true combustion at the level needed to incinerate to ashes while leaving the room or other furnishings undamaged."

The idea of a person spontaneously combusting has long fascinated popular writers. Herman Melville, author of *Moby Dick,* wrote of an inebriated sailor who suddenly bursts into flames in his novel *Redburn,* while Charles Dickens wrote of a man who mysteriously caught on fire and burned to death in his book *Bleak House.*

The rumors of spontaneous human combustion became so widespread in the nineteenth century that the *Chicago Tribune* printed a brief explanation of the phenomenon on August 29, 1875:

The question as to whether there is any such thing as spontaneous combustion of the living human body, is decided by M. Chassagnoil of Brest, after a thorough examination of all the conflicting accounts on record, absolutely in the negative.

Many authors have affirmed that the body, on these occasions of alleged combustion, burned with a blue flame, and diffused an empyreumatic odor, but these characteristics are met with in many kinds of combustion.

Instances have also been sought for by M. Chassagnoil among alcoholic drinkers, especially women, but without success. The idea has been that the alcohol in drinkers takes fire; it is in fact, however, that dead bodies, or portions of dead bodies, burn but very slowly even after having been steeped in alcohol for some days.

The Rooney case, however, has long perplexed investigators. What is known is that on the evening of December 24, 1885, Patrick Rooney and his wife, Matilda, settled in for a night of casual drinking with their hired hand, John Larson. The seventy-two-year-old Patrick Rooney owned and worked a small but prosperous farm located north of Seneca, which is about seventy-five miles southwest of Chicago. He enjoyed a good stiff drink and kept what he called his "little brown jug" of whiskey, which he refilled every week at the saloon of his son-in-law, Michael Murphy, who lived nearby.

According to Larson, he and Mr. and Mrs. Rooney shared a few from the jug that night. After enjoying two drinks, Larson said, he retired to his room, located above the kitchen, and quickly fell asleep.

Sometime during the night he recalled waking up gasping for breath but figured he was just catching a cold and soon drifted off to sleep again. When he awoke the next morning, Larson said he went downstairs to Mr. Rooney's room (the Rooneys slept in separate bedchambers) and found the farmer lying on the floor (or, in some accounts, slumped in a chair).

Concerned that Rooney had passed out after having a few too many drinks, he tried shaking the man so he could help him to his bed. Rooney, however, was unresponsive. Realizing the old man was dead, Larson rushed to Mrs. Rooney's room but found it unoccupied.

Larson's first thought was that the two had quarreled, and Mrs. Rooney had killed her husband and run away. Since the deceased Mr. Rooney wasn't going anywhere and there were chores to be done, Larson took care of his duties before deciding to walk to the nearby Murphy home to tell the family what he thought had happened.

He returned with Michael Murphy, and the two made a thorough search of the house, looking for any indication of where Mrs. Rooney might have gone.

When they passed Larson's upstairs room, they noticed that the pillows were blackened with soot, which Larson realized was probably the reason he had woken up coughing and unable to breathe during the night.

When the two men walked into the kitchen, they finally figured out what had happened to Mrs. Rooney. In the center of the room was a charred and blackened hole that measured several feet wide.

In a story that appeared on January 9, 1886, the local *Ottawa Free Trader* newspaper described the gruesome scene:

> The fire burned a hole just large enough to let Mrs. Rooney's remains fall through . . . the flesh was entirely consumed, except that part which covered the bones of one foot. The [left] foot was found just at the edge of the aperture in the floor, through which the body had disappeared.
>
> The limb had burned slowly to the ankle—flesh and bone—and when the body dropped the charred bone snapped, and the foot, with the shoe intact, righted itself and stood up as if its owner had been burned at the stake. Nothing in the room was burned except Mrs. Rooney's body, the hole in the floor and the table cloth fringe.

On that same day another local paper, *The Ottawa Daily Republican Times*, in equally graphic language noted: "They found a calcined skull, part of a vertebral column and a handful of white ashes beneath the kitchen floor. There was a hole burned though the floor four feet in length and three in breadth through which the incinerated remains had fallen. The walls were blackened as if with lampblack, as was the floor and the woodwork."

The La Salle County coroner, Dr. Floyd Clendenen, was called to the house on Christmas Day. When he arrived, he realized that performing an autopsy on Mrs. Rooney, who had weighed about 160 pounds, was impossible, so he simply collected the bones, bone fragments, and ash, which he cataloged.

In his report Dr. Clendenen wrote that he recovered "the skull, the cervical, and a half the dorsal vertebrae reduced very nearly to a cinder, also about six inches of the right femur, together with part of the ilium [upper portion of the pelvis] in about the same state as the vertebrae."

After studying the scene and the remains, he concluded, "The skull and the hip bone were really the only evidence by which it could be told that a human body had been cremated there."

While he couldn't find an obvious source for the fire, the doctor hypothesized Mrs. Rooney was incinerated by a fire that burned at more than 2,500 degrees Fahrenheit. He also could offer no explanation for how such an intense fire could avoid burning the rest of the kitchen or the house.

In his book, *The Mysterious Fires of ABLAZE! Spontaneous Human Combustion,* author and paranormal investigator Larry E. Arnold, who visited the old Rooney farmhouse in 1993, said he had spoken to a descendent of Mr. and Mrs. Rooney, who told him that over the years many family members have believed that the deaths were the result of "divine retribution" for their excessive drinking on Christmas Eve.

Even the *Ottawa Republican Times* tried to make the same connection, saying, in the headline of a story that appeared on December 31, 1885: "Tragic End of an Old Couple Whose Weakness Was the Cause of Their Sad Demise."

In a letter to the *Free Trader* shortly after the event, one reader stated, "Temperance lecturers have always told stories of the combustion of inebriates . . . theologians would add that the burning must go on eternally."

The belief in a link between spontaneously bursting into flames and drinking large quantities of alcohol was especially popular in the nineteenth century.

For example, the October 14, 1835, issue of the *Boston Medical and Surgical Journal,* in an article titled, "On the Causes of Spontaneous Combustion," pointed out, "The observations which have been hitherto collected in relation to this subject, seem to result in the firm conviction that a very large proportion of those who have suffered from spontaneous combustion, have been addicted to the abusive use of spirituous drinks."

According to the article postmortem examinations of victims of spontaneous combustion showed that a body with high "alcoholic impregnation" had a high degree of combustibility. The article claimed that the blue appearance of the flames in SHC cases were the same as when alcohol is ignited.

In addition, the *Journal* noted other common traits among those who burn up, including the following: They are more likely to be women; they are usually older women, usually more than sixty years old; they live sedentary lives and are bored; they are usually obese; and they abuse alcohol.

According to the article, during spontaneous combustion, which usually occurs in the colder months, the body burns up very rapidly and at very high temperatures. It had also been observed that the internal inferno seemed to originate in the trunk of the body, with exterior limbs, particularly legs and feet, often not burned.

Not surprisingly there is said to be a strong odor of burning organic matter, and afterward the room is covered in dark, greasy soot. With some understatement the report concluded that more research is needed into the subject.

While John Larson was the obvious suspect in the deaths of Mr. and Mrs. Rooney, about a month later the two local Ottawa newspapers reported that he had been exonerated by authorities due to lack of evidence and because he was known to be a man of good character.

After carefully considering the evidence, Dr. Clendenen ruled that "Patrick Rooney had died of smoke inhalation, of that there was little doubt. John Larson escaped death by sleeping behind a closed door on the second floor."

However, the doctor admitted he was at a loss to explain Mrs. Rooney's bizarre demise and could only say she had suffered an accidental death. The coroner offered his opinion of what might have happened when he titled his report, "A Case of Spontaneous Combustion in Man."

Interestingly there have been a handful of other instances of SHC in the Land of Lincoln. One that gained some media attention occurred in September 1949, when fifty-nine-year-old bank janitor Aura Troyer, from Bloomington, died in a mysterious fire.

The People's Bank Building, now known as the Commerce Bank, in downtown Bloomington, Illinois, was once the site of a case of spontaneous human combustion.

According to the *Chicago Tribune,* Troyer was found by a deliveryman in a basement corridor of the New People's Bank in Bloomington on the morning of September 6.

"Only Troyer and his clothing had been burned; nothing in the bank itself or offices in the same building had been disturbed. The origin of the fire could not be determined," the *Tribune* reported.

Unlike most known SHC victims, Troyer was still alive when he was discovered and was rushed to St. Joseph's Hospital. He reportedly uttered, "It happened all of a sudden," just before he expired.

In another case in 1979, fifty-one-year-old Beatrice Oczki, from Bolingbrook, reportedly ignited without provocation and was instantly incinerated. On the night of November 24, Mrs. Oczki said good-bye to her son, who departed for a weekend skiing trip, and then settled into her favorite armchair to drink a beer, smoke a cigarette, and watch television.

Sometime that night the 195-pound Mrs. Oczki, who was diabetic and wore a leg brace, allegedly erupted into flames. According to one account it happened so quickly and with such intensity that the beer in her hand exploded and her two dogs sleeping nearby were instantly asphyxiated.

The fire incinerated the chair in which she was sitting, melted a nearby VCR tape, and blistered the paint on the ceiling above her—but nothing else in the room. The television, still on when she was later found, was undamaged, and a newspaper three feet from her body was unburned.

The next morning Mrs. Oczki's ex-daughter-in-law stopped by the house to pick up a few items and knocked on the door. After getting no response and smelling smoke, she called the fire department.

When the firefighters arrived, they entered the house and discovered a scene that can only be described as horrific. Sticking out from a small pile of ashes and bones were the lower part of two human legs, one wearing a brace.

In their book, *Unexplained Mysteries of the 20th Century*, authors Janet and Colin Bord noted, "Even if Mrs. Oczki was smoking as she watched TV, we are again faced with the mystery of how a cigarette could cause such a conflagration."

How indeed?

CHAPTER 6

Mary, Mary, Quite Contrary

One of the most enduring legends in the Chicagoland area is the story of Resurrection Mary. Her story has appeared in countless books, newspaper stories, and magazine articles—even several television programs.

There are several variations of the Mary myth, but nearly all involve an attractive, young blonde woman dressed in an elegant white gown and dancing shoes who is hitchhiking on Archer Avenue in the southwest Chicago suburb of Justice.

After getting picked up by a male driver, the woman suddenly disappears or, in some versions, requests to be let out at 7201 Archer Avenue—which turns out to be the location of Resurrection Cemetery—where she walks through the gates and vanishes.

While the story is similar to phantom hitchhiker folklore found across the United States, Chicago's Resurrection Mary has had remarkable staying power. One of the earliest articles about the ghost woman of Archer Avenue appeared in the *Chicago Tribune* on May 13, 1974.

"Next time you're driving thru the old South Side Polish neighborhood along Archer Avenue, keep an eye out for Resurrection Mary," the *Tribune* said. "Two generations of Chicagoans claim to have seen her thumbing a ride—a pretty Polish girl, about 18, with long blonde hair, wearing a white dancing dress."

The story quoted Richard T. Crowe, a Chicago "psychic investigator," who told the paper, "Resurrection Mary probably is the most persistent hitchhiking ghost story in Chicago . . . Mary supposedly was killed in a car wreck 40 years ago, and she's been coming back and going dancing ever since."

Crowe, who died in 2012 (and was buried in Resurrection Cemetery), was often described as Chicago's most famous ghost hunter and the foremost expert on Resurrection Mary. From 1973 until his death, he owned and operated Chicago Ghost Tours, which offered bus excursions to haunted locales throughout the Windy City.

According to Crowe's research, Mary's story began in 1939 (although other researchers claim it started in 1936), when a Southside Chicago man named Jerry Palus stopped in at a local dance club, the Liberty Grove Hall and Ballroom, located at 47th Street and Mozart Avenue.

Palus told Crowe that he noticed a very attractive, young blonde woman in a white dancing dress standing across the room. He walked over to the young woman and asked her to dance.

The two tripped the light fantastic for most of the evening, during which Palus learned the girl's name was Mary and she lived in a house on Damen Avenue. He also remembered her as being very quiet and that her skin felt cold. He offered to give her a ride home, which she accepted.

Entrance to the Resurrection Cemetery in Justice, Illinois, said to be the home of the hitchhiking ghost known as Resurrection Mary.

PHOTO BY RICHARD MORENO

However, once they were driving, Mary told him that he might as well take her down to Archer Road, which he thought was peculiar since it was the opposite direction from Damen Avenue.

In a later interview Palus explained: "And I said what for? I said you live up here where you told me. And she says no I want to go out to Archer Road."

Palus said she told him to stop across the street from the front gates leading into Resurrection Cemetery, a large Catholic burial ground that opened in 1907.

He said he asked her if he could walk her somewhere, and she reportedly responded that where she was going he could not follow. Then the young woman opened the car door, sprinted across the road toward the cemetery gates, and seemingly disappeared.

Despite the abrupt end to his date, Palus was taken with the young woman, so the next day he drove to Damen Avenue, to the address where Mary had indicated she lived. He knocked, and a middle-aged woman came to the door. He asked if he could speak to Mary, and the stunned woman told him that her daughter had been dead for five years.

She showed a photo of her daughter to Palus, who recognized her as the same woman he had met in the dance hall.

According to Crowe, "It's then, Jerry said, that he understood why the woman he was dancing with that night was ice cold to the touch. He had worked in a funeral home for awhile and it was the touch of a corpse."

Whenever he was interviewed, Palus, who died in 1992, always insisted the story was true.

According to Chicago author Troy Taylor, who has written dozens of books about ghosts and paranormal activity in the Midwest, Mary has made regular appearances along Archer Avenue over the past seven decades.

In his book, *Haunted Chicago,* Taylor recounted a 1941 encounter with Mary by a Chicago cab driver. The cabbie picked up a young woman who was walking on Archer Avenue late at night.

Despite the winter cold he noticed she was not wearing a coat. She told him she needed to get home quickly but told him to just drive up Archer Avenue.

After a short time, he said, he looked in his rearview mirror to ask her where she wanted to be dropped off, but she was gone. As he continued driving, he noticed that he had just passed the entrance to Resurrection Cemetery.

Another Chicago ghost hunter, Dale Kaczmarek, who is president of the Ghost Research Society, wrote in his book, *Windy City Ghosts,* that Mary is Chicago's most famous ghost.

Kaczmarek shared the experience of a man named Bob Main, reportedly the only known person to have twice encountered Mary.

Late one evening Main was working at a nightclub called Harlow's (now gone) that was located on South Cicero Avenue, a few miles east of Archer Avenue. On two different nights he saw a young woman in the club who behaved strangely. He said she was twenty-four to thirty years old; was about five feet, eight inches tall; was slender; and had long blonde hair.

He said what made him notice her was her extremely pale skin and the old-fashioned curls in her long hair. Her dress also seemed out of place: a faded yellow-white gown that resembled a wedding dress.

Main said the woman didn't dance with anyone but instead kind of whirled around by herself. Whenever anyone would try to speak to her, he said, she just shook her head and stared off, as if her mind was somewhere else.

He said one of the most peculiar things is that both times she appeared, none of his staff could recall ever seeing her enter the club—despite the fact that every customer had to show identification at the door—nor did anyone ever see her leave.

One of the most detailed encounters with Mary happened in January 1979, when another cab driver told *Suburban Trib* columnist Bill Geist of meeting Mary. In the article the driver, who is only identified as Ralph, said he found himself on Archer Avenue around midnight after dropping off a fare, when he spotted a young woman, coatless despite the cold weather, standing beside the road.

"She didn't put out her thumb or nothing like that. She just looked at my cab," Ralph told Geist. "Of course, I stopped, I figured maybe she had car trouble or something."

According to Ralph the woman climbed into his cab. He said she was wearing an elegant white gown, like a disco dress, and "she was a looker. A blonde."

He said he asked her where she was going, and she said she needed to get home. When he tried to get her to be more specific, she seemed confused and simply responded, "The snows came early this year."

Finally, he said, she nodded when he asked her if she wanted him to continue on Archer. "A couple miles up Archer there, she jumped with a start like a horse and said, 'Here! Here!' I hit the brakes," the cab driver said. "I looked around and didn't see no kind of house. 'Where?' I said. And then she sticks her arm and points across the road to my left and says 'There!'

"And that's when it happened. I looked to my left, like this, at this little shack. And when I turned she was gone. Vanished! And the car door never opened. May the good lord strike me dead, it never opened."

Geist reported on a number of other Mary sightings in the 1970s and 1980s, including an incident in August 1976, when a man called the Justice Police Department to report he was driving by Resurrection Cemetery at about ten o'clock at night when he saw a young woman apparently locked inside the gates.

A police car was sent over to investigate but could find no woman. However, the officer did discover something weird: Two of the bars on the cemetery's bronze fence were bent as if they had been pulled apart, and he could see what looked like handprints burned into the metal.

According to Geist, the cemetery "denied the story emphatically," claiming the bent bars were the result of a collision with a front-end loader truck and the handprints were created when a workman tried to use a blowtorch to soften the metal bars and grabbed them with asbestos gloves.

There have been additional sightings in more recent years, including several reports in the early 1980s and 1990s. According to Troy Taylor, one involved a young man who on September 5, 1980, was driving on Archer Avenue after playing softball with friends. He noticed an attractive young woman in a white dress standing beside the road and pulled over to offer her a ride.

She accepted and told him she just wanted a ride down Archer Avenue. He tried to engage her in conversation and offered to buy her a drink, but she didn't reply.

As he passed Resurrection Cemetery, he turned to ask her one more time where she wanted to go, but she was gone.

Several encounters have occurred near a local bar, Chet's Melody Lounge (7400 South Archer Road). In a number of the accounts, a confused and perplexed male driver stumbled into Chet's for a drink after having picked up a young woman in white who mysteriously disappeared from the car.

In a few cases the driver said he believed he had accidently hit a young woman who just appeared in the middle of Archer Avenue, but later he could find no body.

So who was Mary the mystery hitchhiker, and why have people seen her hanging out in dance halls or wandering around Archer Avenue?

According to most versions of the popular legend, Mary was a young woman who, sometime in the 1930s, went to a dance at the Oh Henry Ballroom (now known as the Willowbrook Ballroom, located at 8900 Archer Avenue), where she spent most of the evening dancing with her boyfriend.

The two, however, got into an argument and Mary left the hall. She decided that even though it was a cold evening, she would rather walk home than have to spend any more time with her boyfriend.

Apparently she began walking on Archer Avenue but was struck by a car. The driver took off, leaving her to die by the side of the road.

Her body was discovered by her parents, who had her buried at Resurrection Cemetery, dressed in an elegant white dancing dress with matching shoes. It's believed she haunts Archer Avenue and nearby dance halls because the driver who killed her was never found.

But is that the whole story? Not entirely, say a number of Mary aficionados. Writer and ghost tour guide Ursula Bielski, author of *Chicago Haunts: Ghostlore of the Windy City*, has extensively studied the Resurrection Mary mythology and concluded that Mary did exist and it's a strong possibility her real name was Anna Marija Norkus (a religious girl, Anna apparently called herself by her middle name, which translates to Mary).

According to Bielski, on July 20, 1927, the blonde and vivacious Anna, who loved to dance, begged her father, August, to take her to a ballroom in advance of her birthday. He agreed, even though she was only turning thirteen (apparently she was pretty mature for her age).

They went to the Oh Henry Ballroom, where they danced and had a good time until late into the evening. On the drive home they passed Resurrection Cemetery and then turned onto 71st Street before heading north on Harlem Avenue to 67th Street.

Unfortunately, on that night the Chicago Streets Department, which had been doing work on the road, neglected to put up proper signage warning motorists there was a recently uncovered, nearly invisible twenty-five-foot-deep railroad cut in the street. Anna's father did not see the huge hole in the road and plunged right into it. He and several other passengers survived, but Anna was crushed to death.

As for why Anna has remained a wandering spirit, Bielski theorized that while she was originally supposed to be buried in the St. Casimir Cemetery, it was common in those days for gravediggers to go on strike and during those times for bodies to be temporarily buried in one of the city's nonstriking cemeteries. She said it was possible that Anna's body was temporarily buried at nearby Resurrection Cemetery.

"It is quite possible that young Anna Norkus was silently whisked to a temporary internment at Resurrection, and that a rapid decomposition rendered her unidentifiable at the time of exhumation," she wrote. "The result? A mislaid corpse and a most restless entity."

Some investigators, however, argue that Anna couldn't possibly be Mary, because she's far too young. Additionally it's not clear that Anna was buried at Resurrection Cemetery but actually might have been interred someplace else.

Others who have studied Mary have suggested another candidate: a woman named Mary Bregovy, who died in a tragic automobile accident in March 1934. Bregovy, who was twenty-one when she died, is closer in age to the woman described in Resurrection Mary encounters, and she lived on Damen Avenue.

Additionally, Bregovy was buried in Resurrection Cemetery in what is called a term grave, meaning that her plot was sold on a twenty-five-year term. When the term expired, her family would be asked to renew the lease or the marker would be removed and the land resold for a new grave.

No doubt this could result in a pretty agitated ghost.

Detractors, however, note that Bregovy had short, brown hair and the location of her car accident was uptown near Lake Street and Wacker Drive—nowhere near Archer Avenue—so it was unlikely she was returning home from an evening of dancing at the Oh Henry Ballroom.

Yet another name associated with the legend is Mary Miskowski, said to be a blonde eighteen- or nineteen-year-old Southside Chicago woman who was hit by a car and killed on

October 31, 1930, while crossing the street on her way to a Halloween party.

Most dismiss this Mary's claim to being Resurrection Mary because no death records or accident reports involving anyone by that name during that period have ever been found.

In the end perhaps the late Richard Crowe had it right when he told a *Chicago Tribune* reporter in 1992 that "Mary doesn't seem to be one person."

But is she real? When asked if he thought the legend of Resurrection Mary could be true, Rich Prusinski, longtime manager of Chet's Melody Lounge, who has met many of those who claimed to have encountered Mary, told a newspaper reporter: "I don't know—I've never seen the wind, but I know that it's there."

CHAPTER 7

The Horror

Undoubtedly the most nightmarish entity ever to crawl, shamble, or in this case, hop across the Illinois landscape was the bizarre creature that became known as the Enfield Horror.

The monstrosity was allegedly first sighted at about 8:30 p.m. on April 25, 1973. A ten-year-old boy named Gary Garrett was startled by a strange animal that appeared while he was playing in the yard of his parents' home in the small southern Illinois town of Enfield (population about 600). According to the terrified youngster, the thing was about four feet tall, slimy, and gray with pink or reddish eyes. He said it had only three legs and sharp-clawed feet.

The weird beast apparently hopped toward the boy and landed on his sneaker, which was easily shredded by the claws. The hysterical boy said he scampered into the house and told his parents he had been attacked by something, but by the time they investigated, the monster was gone.

And that's probably where the story would have ended if not for another, very similar experience about a half hour later. This time Henry McDaniel, a disabled war veteran and neighbor of the Garrett family, returned home to find his two children, Henry Jr. and Lil, scared out of their wits.

The children said some kind of strange animal had been trying to claw its way into the house. McDaniel then heard scratching at his front door and went to investigate.

He opened the door and saw, on his front stoop, a weird-looking creature that resembled the thing seen earlier that night by Gary Garrett.

"When I first saw it, I thought it was an animal. I went back [inside the house] and got a gun and a flashlight," he later told reporters. "It was right about three feet from me, I wasn't scared. Then I saw those pink eyes shine at me like a reflector on a car. It had pink eyes, a large head, and was a kind of dirtyish gray color . . . hairy . . . about four or five feet tall. Standing right in front of the door on three legs just like a human being."

McDaniel said he fired several shots at the animal, hitting it at least once. He told police that it didn't fall to the ground or seem wounded but began hissing at him like an angry cat.

Then, he said, the most amazing thing occurred. The beast turned and leaped about seventy-five feet in three long jumps. It vanished in the tall brush along a railroad embankment behind his house.

"I'd like to have it as a pet and charge admission," he later joked to the media. "It's something that's there and we got to accept it."

After his encounter with the creature, McDaniel immediately called the police, and two state troopers responded. They investigated the house and surroundings but found little to corroborate his story, except for odd scratch marks on his door and windowsills as well as prints in the dirt that resembled those of a large dog—albeit a three-legged dog with six toe pads.

However, a May 7 United Press International story noted that Ed Phillips, a pet shop owner from Kokomo, Indiana, came out to look at the scratches and footprints. "It couldn't be a hoax," Phillips said, adding that he had also seen the weird tracks around the house and under the dense brush adjacent to the railroad tracks.

In a 1978 article on the theory of social contagion (the idea that masses of people in certain circumstances will adopt irrational or hysterical behavior) in the *Sociological Quarterly,* authors David L. Miller, Kenneth J. Mietus, and Richard A. Mathers of Western Illinois University decided to focus on what exactly had happened in Enfield in 1973.

They closely studied media accounts about the episode, including those reported in the local newspaper, the *Carmi Times,* as well as by radio station WWKI of nearby Kokomo, Indiana, and in newspapers throughout the Midwest.

For example, on April 27 McDaniel told the *Champaign-Urbana News Gazette*—which made a point of telling its readers how rational and sober he was in an apparent attempt to show he wasn't crazy—that several local schoolchildren had seen a similar animal near the school ballpark. He said he believed there could be more than one of the creatures and offered: "They were not from this planet."

The episode wasn't the last time McDaniel said he caught sight of the strange entity. Late at night on May 6, he was awoken by the frenetic barks of several neighborhood dogs. Curious, he climbed out of bed, once again picked up a flashlight and his pistol, and opened his front door.

There, several yards away, was the gray three-legged creature again. This time it was casually hopping over the nearby railroad tracks. McDaniel said he didn't feel threatened by the creature, so he didn't fire his gun. After a short time the beast headed away along the rails.

"It wasn't in a hurry or anything," he later told authorities.

In addition to McDaniel's sightings, radio station WWKI's news director, Rick Rainbow, and three companions said that same day, May 6, they observed an "ape-like" animal prowling around an old barn near McDaniel's home. They crept near the creature and recorded tape of what they claimed was its strange wail, and then fired off a shot that scared it away. Later accounts said the creature made a noise similar to an elephant's call.

Researchers Miller, Mietus, and Mathers traveled to Enfield about two weeks after the initial sighting in 1973 to investigate the reports. They noted that the media stories had attracted the

attention of a number of armed, often inebriated "monster hunters," many of whom were quickly arrested by local authorities for
violating state and local hunting ordinances.

They speculated that the real danger to Enfield residents
wasn't the possibility of meeting the strange three-legged creature
but accidentally running into a drunken armed hunter. Despite
the increased presence of people trying to either see or capture
the monster, there were no further sightings.

Miller, Mietus, and Mathers interviewed many of the
people who claimed to have seen the creature and discovered that
in at least one case the report was "an ill-advised practical joke."
The story of the creature's attack on young Gary Garrett turned
out to be a fabrication.

"Our interview with the boy and his parents disclosed
they invented the 'shoe tearing' episode to 'tease' their eccentric
neighbor [McDaniel] and to have some fun with an out of town
newsman," they wrote.

The researchers, however, didn't discount McDaniel's report
of events, nor did they find anything to indicate the radio station
crew's claim that they had encountered the thing was not true.

According to several accounts McDaniel eventually was
warned to stop talking about his brush with the bizarre by the local
sheriff, who allegedly threatened to lock him in jail if he continued
to speak to the media because he was riling up the public.

In their article Miller, Mietus, and Mathers wrote that
the sheriff was "perhaps the most vehement in his denial that a

monster had been sighted." They added that he may have felt
that way because his normal work routine had been disrupted
the most from having to deal with the influx of armed would-be
monster killers, as well as the media and worried local residents.

So what really happened during late April and early
May 1973? Loren Coleman, who is often described as one of
America's foremost "cryptozoologists" (someone who studies animals whose existence has yet to be proven) was taking
anthropology and zoology courses at the University of Illinois at
Champaign-Urbana at the time and decided to travel to Enfield
to investigate.

In a May 12, 1973, story in the Robinson (Illinois) *Daily
News,* then–twenty-five-year-old Coleman is quoted as saying he
believed the creature was some kind of anthropoid ape.

"These are not the first such monster reports and they
won't be the last," he told the newspaper.

Of his visit to Enfield, Coleman later wrote: "I interviewed
the witnesses, looked at the siding and air conditioner damage of
the house the Enfield Monster had attacked, heard some strange
screeching banshee-like sounds, and walked away bewildered."

Coleman also told the media that there had been previous
reports of similar apelike animals in other parts of the country
and in Illinois. He mentioned an episode with some kind of
monkey animal in Canton, Alabama, in 1960, as well as reports
of an apelike thing in other parts of southern Illinois, including
one near Bridgeport in 1962 and another in Jackson County

in 1942. During the latter encounter the monster was said to have hopped twenty to forty feet across highways, much like Enfield's creature.

He also recounted the story of Reverend Lepton Harpole, who, in the summer of 1941, ran into some kind of monkey or apelike creature in the woods near Mount Vernon, Illinois. Reverend Harpole was hunting squirrels along the Gum Creek bottom when he reported seeing "a large animal that looked something like a baboon," which he said startled him when it leapt from a tree and knocked off his hat.

He said he swatted at the strange animal with the barrel of his shotgun and then fired off a shot in the air, which frightened it. The thing scampered off into the forest and wasn't seen again.

In their book, *The Unidentified & Creatures of the Outer Edge,* Coleman and coauthor Jerome Clark noted that a few months after the Mount Vernon incident there were a number of other odd occurrences in the region, generally in the wooded bottomlands near local creeks and rivers.

For instance, they said people reported finding unusual tracks and a farm dog was found mauled by some unknown animal near the small hamlet of Bonnie, Illinois, located about twenty miles south of Mount Vernon. In the latter case, hunting parties quickly formed to capture or kill the beast but, according to Coleman and Clark, "The creature easily evaded them (perhaps because of its reputed ability to leap twenty to forty feet in a single bound)."

In the early 1970s there were a series of unexplained sightings, including in the central Illinois community of Farmer City (located about thirty miles northwest of Champaign), where a number of hogs and sheep were found slashed to death and witnesses spotted a creature that ran on two legs and had strange glowing eyes.

Shortly after that occurrence, a Bloomington, Illinois, woman reported encountering what she first thought was a dog, but when she looked more closely, "I saw this ape running in the ditch. The thing I saw was the size of a baboon."

As for what the Enfield creature might have been, one online site has claimed that the monster was a visitor from another world—an alien life-form that arrived via a flying saucer or some other type of extraterrestrial vehicle. Not surprisingly this allegation came during a time when the Southern Illinois region was experiencing a rash of supposed UFO sightings.

Others, on the other hand, have speculated that the Enfield phantom was perhaps some kind of mutated ape, which a few have referred to as the "devil monkey." Still others have said it was an escaped kangaroo or wallaby (although no one is quite sure where it would have escaped from).

In their book Coleman and Clark discounted the marsupial theory, noting that when they interviewed Henry McDaniel following his experience, he emphatically said: "I've been all around this world. I've been through Africa and I've had a pet kangaroo.

This was not a kangaroo. I've never seen this type of creature or track before."

As with most news events, within a short time the media moved on to cover other stories—the Watergate scandal was just beginning to come to light and Vice President Spiro Agnew would resign later that year.

In Enfield, life returned to normal and Henry McDaniel slipped back into obscurity. There were no further reports of anyone seeing any more weird, gray, three-legged hopping creatures.

Or at least not yet. The website www.americanmonsters .com has suggested that perhaps the Enfield monster hibernates between its appearances, which seem to occur about every three or four decades, based on anecdotal evidence and eyewitness accounts.

"While there are no reputable accounts of the creature hailing from the 21st century, one cannot entirely count out the possibility that the thing is a long slumbering anatomical oddity that rears its head every so often to feed on animals and terrify locals," noted the site. "Whatever this creature is or is not, it has not been reported in almost 40 years."

Maybe it is time for another close encounter of the three-legged kind.

CHAPTER 8

Accidental Shooting or Assassination?

There are two wildly divergent narratives regarding the shooting death of Chicago mayor Anton Cermak in February 1933.

In the official version of the story, the popular mayor was the accidental victim of Giuseppe Zangara, a lone and most likely insane gunman who was actually trying to assassinate President-elect Franklin D. Roosevelt, but hit Cermak and several others when his arm was jostled.

The other theory, however, is far more sinister. It suggests Zangara was a front man for the Chicago mob and his target was Cermak, who just a few months earlier had ordered an unsuccessful hit on mob boss Frank Nitti, the successor to Al Capone.

A February 1950 FBI memo on the Cermak shooting succinctly summarized the official view of the shooting:

Giuseppe Zangara, Italian-born, naturalized American citizen, on February 15, 1933, at Miami, Florida, shot into a crowd which included, among others, President-elect Franklin D. Roosevelt.

86

Five individuals, including Mayor Anton J. Cermak of Chicago, were wounded. Mr. Roosevelt escaped injury. Zangara was indicted under local charges and after pleading guilty on February 20, 1933, was given an eighty-year sentence, twenty years each on four charges of attempted murder. On March 6, 1933, Mayor Cermak died. Zangara was then indicted for first-degree murder, to which he pleaded guilty. On March 20, 1933, he was electrocuted by the State of Florida.

In this version of the story, Giuseppe Zangara was an unemployed, itinerant bricklayer with some peculiar political views. He was born on September 7, 1900 in the province of Calabria, Italy. When he was two years old, his mother died and he was raised by his father, Salvatore, a hard, unemotional man who, Zangara claimed, regularly beat him.

Zangara said his father had no use for education and refused to allow him to attend school. Instead, Salvatore Zangara, a farmer who was frequently away from home earning money, expected young Giuseppe to work in the fields and care for the family stock animals.

Throughout his life, Zangara said, he suffered persistent stomach pain—an autopsy following his death showed he had a chronically diseased gall bladder—which he blamed on the fact that his father had made him work so hard as a child.

During World War I, the diminutive Zangara—he was only slightly taller than five feet—worked as a laborer building trenches in Northern Italy and was trained as a stonemason.

In 1923 he applied for a visa to move to America, which he did in August of that year. Once he arrived, he moved in with an uncle, Vincent Carfaro, who lived in Brooklyn, New York. Within a short time the two men relocated to Paterson, New Jersey, where Zangara began working as a bricklayer.

After finding out he needed to join a union to continue working, which required applying to be a US citizen, Zangara filed for citizenship. Six years later, on September 11, 1929, he was sworn in as an American citizen. About a month later the US stock market crashed, and the country was plunged into the Great Depression.

By 1931, construction jobs had become so scarce that Zangara could no longer pay his union dues and he did not work much. He had, however, begun to travel around the United States, apparently living off of money he had saved.

It's known that in late 1929, Zangara visited Florida and then traveled to New Orleans. After returning to New Jersey, he went back to New Orleans, where he stayed for several months.

In the spring of 1931, Zangara traveled to California by ship (via the Panama Canal), where he lived for nearly a year. In February 1932 the peripatetic Zangara returned to Florida because, he later said, the warm weather made his stomach feel better. A few months later he was back in New Jersey before relocating once again to Miami in August 1932.

Over time Zangara began to obsess about shooting the president of the United States. He blamed his constant stomach pain on the fact that he had been forced to work at a young age because his father didn't have the money to send him to school. He believed that the source of his problems was the capitalist economic system and its leaders, particularly the president.

"That way I make my idea to kill the president," he later said. "Kill any president, king, and I have a machine gun in my hand—I will kill all president and king, and all capitalist and everything they take."

Zangara claimed that in the early 1920s he had tried to assassinate King Victor Emmanuel III of Italy but failed because he couldn't get close enough, although there is some doubt about that claim.

It's also been reported that sometime in late 1932 he tried to kill President Herbert Hoover, Roosevelt's predecessor, but abandoned the plan after waiting outside the White House gates for ten days.

It is known that sometime in early February 1933, Zangara purchased a used, nickel-plated .32 caliber five-shot revolver and ten bullets from a downtown Miami pawnshop.

A few days later, on February 15, he neatly packed all of his possessions into a small, inexpensive suitcase, which he laid on his bed in the attic room he rented in a Miami house.

In addition to his clothing, the valise contained three grammar and language books and a handful of newspaper clippings about President Roosevelt's visit to Miami. Zangara walked to Bayfront Park, where Roosevelt would be speaking that evening.

At about nine o'clock Roosevelt, who had been on a two-week fishing trip in the Caribbean aboard a yacht owned by wealthy businessman Vincent Astor, climbed into a green Buick convertible and headed from the yacht toward the park, where a crowd of about ten thousand people had gathered to hear the man who would soon become their president. As his small motorcade traveled the short distance, Roosevelt waved and smiled to people lining the streets.

About an hour and a half earlier, Zangara had arrived at the park bandstand, in front of which Roosevelt would be speaking (the president's convertible was to park in front of the bandstand). He pushed his way through the crowd, stopping at the third row from the front when it became obvious that he could get no closer.

Several local notables, including the mayor of Miami, Redmond Gautier, welcomed the president-elect to Miami. When the time came for Roosevelt to talk, he was helped to a position atop the backseat of the open convertible and handed a microphone. He thanked everyone for coming and spoke very briefly about his recent fishing trip and how happy he was to be in Miami, but he said nothing more substantive.

After less than a minute, he handed the microphone back to Gautier and was helped down into the backseat of the car. Following the speech a small group of dignitaries surrounded Roosevelt's car, including Mayor Cermak, who had traveled to Miami specifically to speak to the president-elect about federal assistance for his city. According to a February 16 story in the *Chicago Tribune,* the two men shook hands warmly and Roosevelt said, "Hello there, Mr. Mayor. How are you?"

Because of all the noise, the two men bent their heads together to talk. At that moment Zangara decided to act. He climbed onto a chair, pulled out his revolver, and fired five shots.

"Suddenly two shots rang out," the *Tribune* reported. "L.L. Lee, city manager of Miami, who had his arm linked in Mayor Cermak's at the moment, said the mayor sagged but did not fall. Mr. Cermak turned around slightly, looking for [Alderman James] Bowler. Seeing him five feet behind, he called out, 'I'm hit, Jim.'"

The story noted that at first no one seemed to understand what had happened, as most in the crowd thought the shots were the popping noise of photographers' flashbulbs. However, after three more shots were fired, Roosevelt's driver quickly gleaned what was going on and started up the car.

As the car began to accelerate to get the president-elect away from the shooting, Alderman Bowler yelled to Roosevelt that Cermak had been shot. The president-elect ordered his car to stop so that Cermak could be quickly placed into the car, then, "with sirens screaming, but with a different purpose this time than to let people know their next President was approaching, the car sped about twenty blocks to the Jackson Memorial hospital," the *Tribune* reported.

In addition to shooting Cermak, Zangara injured four others, including Margaret Kruis of New Jersey, who was shot through the hand; Russell Caldwell of Miami, who received a head wound from a deflected bullet; William Sinnott, a New York police officer, who also received a slight head wound; and Mabel Gill of Miami, who was seriously injured by a gunshot in the stomach.

Immediately after the shots were fired, several police officers and members of the crowd rushed Zangara and wrestled him to the ground. During the struggle one officer hit Zangara repeatedly with a blackjack and his clothing was ripped from his body. Within a few minutes the police had apprehended the beaten Zangara and pulled him away from the crowd.

Concerned that someone in the crowd might try to kill him, they quickly laid Zangara out on the trunk of a police car and strapped him to a luggage rack, with two police officers sitting on him, and rushed him to the Dade County Jail.

Once he was booked for the shootings, Zangara was given a quick examination by the county doctor and then stripped of his remaining clothing and locked in a cell. He was questioned by Dade County Sheriff Dan Hardie as well as Secret Service agents and other law enforcement officials.

Additionally, several reporters were allowed to speak to the prisoner, including one from the *Chicago Tribune,* who quoted Zangara as saying in broken English: "As a man I like Meester Roosevelt. As a president I want to keel him. I want to keel all presidents. In Italy ten years ago I want to keel the king. But I cannot get to heem."

According to the *Tribune,* when Zangara was pressed by authorities to acknowledge he was an anarchist or a communist,

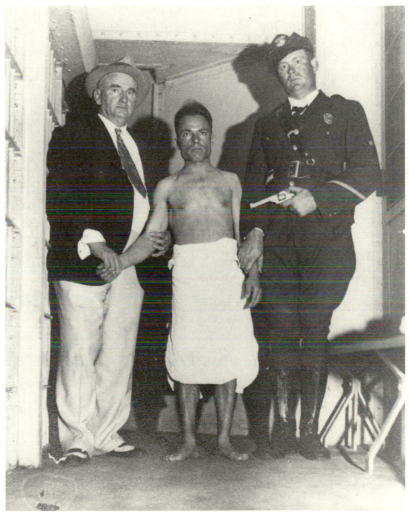

Accused assassin Giuseppe Zangara poses with Florida lawmen after being arrested for the attempted assassination of Chicago mayor Anton Cermak and President Franklin D. Roosevelt on February 15, 1933.

STATE LIBRARY AND ARCHIVES OF FLORIDA

93

he responded: "I do not belong to any society. I am no anarchist. Sometimes I get a beeg pain in my stomach, too, and then I want to keel these presidents who oppress the workingman."

Less than twelve hours after the assassination attempt on Roosevelt, Zangara was taken to court for arraignment on four counts of attempted murder. He was charged with attempted murder, and a grand jury was convened specifically to charge Zangara with murder should one of his victims die.

After the charges were read to him, Zangara was asked if he understood them and if he wanted a lawyer. After he indicated he did understand but wanted no legal representation, Judge E. C. Collins decided he would appoint one anyway and deferred the decision to the following day.

In court the next day, Judge Collins appointed three prominent Miami attorneys—none, however, with much experience in criminal law cases—to stand with Zangara and ordered a psychiatric evaluation.

A few days later Zangara appeared before Judge Collins and pleaded guilty to the four charges. During a brief interview with the judge, Zangara repeated his grievances against President Roosevelt and the capitalist system and said his only regret was that he did not kill the president. In response, Judge Collins declared Zangara guilty of all charges and sentenced him to four consecutive sentences of twenty years of hard labor.

About three weeks after the shooting, on March 6, Mayor Cermak, who had appeared to rally a few days earlier, took a turn for the worse and died. The grand jury immediately indicted Zangara for first-degree murder and, two weeks after receiving an eighty-year sentence, he was back in court before Judge Oly O. Thompson.

Again he pleaded guilty, stating, "I want to kill the president because I no like the capitalists. I have the gun in my hand. I kill kings and presidents first and next all capitalists."

On March 10 Judge Thompson ordered the state of Florida to execute Zangara. Three days later Florida governor David Sholtz signed the death warrant and set the week of March 20 for the execution at the Florida Prison Farm at Raiford, Florida.

On the first day of that week, Monday, March 20, Zangara was seated and strapped into a straight-backed wooden chair that was bolted to the floor. A sponge woven with copper wires and soaked in salt water was placed on top of a shaved spot on his head and held in place by a leather strap that went under his chin. A black hood was placed over his head.

After an electric motor was turned on and began to hum, an anxious but defiant Zangara shouted out, "Viva Italia! Goodbye to all poor people anywhere! Pusha da button! Go ahead, pusha da button!"

At about 9:15 a.m., the switch was thrown and twenty-three hundred volts of electricity raced through Zangara's body. He was pronounced dead at 9:27 a.m.

Justice had been swift; the Bayfront Park shootings had occurred only thirty-three days earlier.

But is that the whole story? Some believe the official version of events is bunk. For example, investigative reporter John W. Tuohy, author of *Capone's Mob Murdered Roger Touhy*, has written that President Roosevelt was never in Zangara's pistol sight—the real target was Mayor Cermak.

According to Tuohy, Cermak and his ally, gangster Roger Touhy (no relation to the author), were locked in a death struggle with the Al Capone/Frank Nitti mob for control of Chicago's vice industries.

In mid-December 1932 Cermak had attempted to have Nitti killed (Capone was already in prison for tax evasion), using two crooked Chicago detectives, who shot Nitti six times. Unfortunately for Cermak, however, Nitti didn't die.

"They had to kill him (Cermak)," Tuohy wrote. "Murdering Cermak was the key. Kill the head and the body dies."

Tuohy said the best way to accomplish the hit was to find someone expendable and not directly connected to the Capone outfit. Additionally, he wrote, "the syndicate knew the shooter they found would have to be a 'nutcase.'"

Enter Zangara, who Tuohy described as a "mean, near-illiterate, sullen little hood from Southern Italy."

While the FBI and law enforcement records showed Zangara had no criminal record nor known associations with criminals, Tuohy's sources claim Zangara had once operated an illegal whiskey still in New Jersey during Prohibition and, while living in Florida, had become a heavy gambler (in horse racing) who soon owed a lot of money to the mob.

To help pay off his debts, Zangara allegedly became a drug courier, smuggling heroin between Florida and New York. During one of his runs, Zangara supposedly took the cash he was supposed to bring back to Florida and lost it at the track.

According to Tuohy, Zangara was given two choices: "The mob could kill him, or Zangara could take his chances and shoot Cermak for them . . . Zangara chose to kill Cermak and take his chances with an insanity plea or the possibility that he could slip into the crowd and disappear."

The Chicago mob, however, didn't want or expect Zangara to live. Their hope was that Miami police or the Secret Service would shoot him dead. Failing that, according to Tuohy, the gangsters had two mob assassins hidden in the crowd to shoot Zangara immediately after he killed Cermak.

Fortunately for Zangara the two shooters were unable to get a clear shot at him during the confusion that erupted after he fired his shots.

In his definitive book about the reach of the Chicago mob, *The Outfit,* writer Gus Russo echoed Tuohy's version of events. He quoted Municipal Judge John Lyle, who he described as one of Chicago's most aggressive antimob jurists during the 1930s, saying, "Zangara was a Mafia killer, sent from Sicily to do a job and sworn to silence."

Additionally Russo noted that President Roosevelt was at one end of the stage while Mayor Cermak was at the other end when Zangara began firing shots in Cermak's direction.

"William Sinnott, a New York policeman injured in the attack, said, 'He was no more shooting at Mr. Roosevelt than I was,'" Russo wrote. "Mark Wilcox, a Florida congressman who witnessed the shooting, stated emphatically, 'He was shooting at Cermak. There is no doubt about that. The killer waited until Mr. Roosevelt sat down and then fired.' For his part, Roosevelt agreed with the other eyewitnesses that he was not the target. For the rest of his life he reiterated the opinion that Zangara was 'a Chicago gangster' hired to take out Cermak."

A related hypothesis, advanced by Chicago writer and community organizer Saul Alinsky, a friend of Nitti's, is that Zangara never actually shot Cermak—he was simply a syndicate patsy who could credibly take the fall for the real killer.

The shooter, according to Alinsky, was one of the mob assassins in the crowd, who allegedly picked off Cermak during the melee that followed Zangara's shots.

Who was the real target? The Mafia has a code of silence known as "omerta," meaning no one may speak about the group's actions and activities under the threat of death. It also means we'll probably never know the entire story.

CHAPTER 9

Possession in Watseka

Mary Lurancy "Rancy" Vennum had a unique ability—it's said she could communicate with the dead.

Born on April 16, 1864, in Milford Township, located seven miles south of Watseka, Illinois, Lurancy, who became known as the "Watseka Wonder," began experiencing strange visions and seizures when she was thirteen years old.

According to Dr. E. Winchester Stevens, who examined her and wrote about her case, in early July 1877 Lurancy began seeing (or feeling the presence of) people in her room when she tried to sleep.

"There were persons in my room last night, and they called, 'Rancy! Rancy!' and I felt their breath on my face," she told her family.

A few days after that experience, Lurancy said she didn't feel well following a daylong session of sewing with her mother, and she fell to the floor. Dr. Stevens wrote that the young woman lay there completely rigid for more than five hours before reviving and saying she felt "very strange and queer."

The same thing occurred the next day, except this time she began to speak, telling her family that she could see a variety of deceased family members and friends, even describing them and calling them by name.

"Oh mother! Can't you see little Laura and Bertie? They are so beautiful," she said, referring to two siblings who had passed away when Lurancy was very young.

For the next month Lurancy continued to have these episodes or trances, during which she described a place she called heaven as well as various spiritlike entities, which she said were angels.

These bouts ended for a time in September and October, but shortly after Thanksgiving in 1877, she complained of horrible stomach pains—often five or six times per day—during which she would double herself backward until, according to Stevens, "her head and feet actually touched."

On December 11 she fell into another stupor and, once again, spoke of being in heaven, surrounded by the angel spirits. This pattern of moving into and out of a dreamlike state continued for another month and a half.

Of course almost as soon as she began behaving in such an odd way, her concerned parents had asked local doctors to examine her and come up with a cure for her mysterious ailment. According to Stevens the doctors were concerned about her mental health, and several of her relatives as well as the local minister believed she needed to be admitted to an insane asylum.

As all of this was happening, the Roff family, also of Watseka, learned of Lurancy's condition and recognized that something similar had occurred with their daughter exactly twelve years before.

The Roffs were not closely acquainted with the Vennums and, in fact, lived on the other side of the town, which at that time had a population of about 1,550.

The head of the Roff family, Asa B. Roff, was a successful businessman and lawyer who had built the first wood-frame home in Watseka in the late 1850s. About a decade later he erected the first brick house ever constructed in the community on a parcel located at 300 E. Sheridan Street.

Asa Roff also was a devout Spiritualist, a then-popular movement in the United States that included a belief that the living could communicate with the dead and that most diseases had spiritual origins. He and his wife were concerned that Lurancy Vennum's doctors would, in the words of Stevens, "take a lovely child from the bosom of an affectionate family, to imprison her among maniacs, to be ruled and cared for by ignorant and bigoted strangers, who know less of catalepsy than a blind materialist does of immortality."

With that in mind Asa Roff contacted Stevens, who was a well-known Spiritualist doctor as well as a medical physician (and a hypnotist), and persuaded him to join him in trying to help the Vennum girl.

The Roff family had become acquainted with Stevens, who lived in Janesville, Wisconsin, after their own daughter, Mary, experienced strange convulsions that ultimately led to her death.

When she was only six months old, Mary Roff, who was born on October 8, 1846, began having small seizures every few weeks. According to accounts the pupils of her eyes would dilate and her muscles would contract and twitch for several moments. As she grew older, the fits became more violent and frequent, and, not surprisingly, Mary would become very depressed.

When she was fifteen, her parents sought medical help—including leeches applied to her temples and hydrotherapy—but doctors could find no explanation or cure for her condition.

At the age of eighteen, a despondent Mary took a knife and slashed her arm in several places, which caused so much bleeding that she fainted. When she awoke, she "became a raving maniac of the most violent kind," according to Stevens, who added that it took five men to hold her down. She remained in this agitated state for much of the next five days.

After Mary finally calmed, she appeared not to recognize any of her family members or friends. Stevens said she had lost her senses of sight, hearing, and feeling. Yet despite that, she could read, dress herself, and walk around the room while wearing a blindfold.

"She could . . . do everything as readily as when in health by her natural sight," he wrote. "She would dress, stand before the glass, open and search drawers, pick up loose pins, do any and all things readily and without annoyance, under heavy blindfoldings."

He also recounted a time when a blindfolded Mary Roff sat and read from a box of letters and even sorted them so that they were all facing the same direction.

After a brief respite, however, the fits resumed, and, in 1865, Mary was committed to the Illinois State Asylum in Peoria for treatment.

On July 5 of that year, Mary's parents visited her in Peoria. The reunion went well, with Mary in good spirits. However, following breakfast, she said she wasn't feeling well and went to bed.

MARY LURANCY VENNUM.

Portrait of Mary Lurancy Vennum, who, as a thirteen-year-old, was said to have been possessed by the spirit of another young woman who had died twelve years earlier.

A few minutes later she screamed and started convulsing. After several minutes she suddenly stopped struggling and died. She was nineteen years old.

Lurancy Vennum's family agreed that Asa Roff and Dr. Stevens could examine their daughter. On January 31, 1878, the two men arrived at the Vennum house to meet and observe the girl. When they entered, they found her curled in a chair next to a stove.

She silently stared at the two men until Dr. Stevens moved his chair to get a closer look at her. She sternly told him to stay away and began insulting members of her family, calling her father, "Old Black Dick," and her grandmother, "Old Granny."

She would not allow anyone to touch her—initially refusing to even shake hands with either man—before finally acknowledging Dr. Stevens, saying she would talk to him because he was a Spiritual doctor.

During the conversation, Lurancy told the doctor that her name was "Katrina Hogan" and that she was sixty-three years old. As the conversation continued, the girl's demeanor changed, and she told the doctor that her real name was "Willie Canning," a young man who had run away from home. She began to pepper the doctor with questions about whether he had any children, had ever traveled around the world and where, and ever drank, smoked, stole, or swore.

After several hours the two men rose to leave, but Lurancy fell to the floor where she lay rigid and stiff. Dr. Stevens clutched the girl's hands, and the two began to talk. Lurancy told Dr. Stevens that she was in heaven. She said there were a number of spirits or angels with her, some good and some bad.

The doctor urged her to seek out the most positive spirits, which she said she would do. After naming and describing several of those around her—all of whom were deceased—she said there was one in particular who wanted to meet them, one who was named Mary Roff.

Asa Roff immediately said that was his daughter and urged Lurancy to "let her come."

According to Stevens, "Lurancy, after due deliberations and counsel with spirits, said that Mary would take the place of the former wild and unreasonable influence."

The following day Thomas Vennum, Lurancy's father, visited Asa Roff at his office and told him that Lurancy now insisted she was Mary Roff and had asked to be taken home (to the Roff's house) because she was homesick.

The Vennums sought to comfort their daughter, who no longer experienced seizures, but she was adamant that she did not know them (although she would eventually regard them as good friends) and wanted to be taken home.

About a week later Mrs. Ann Roff and her daughter, Mrs. Minerva Alter (Mary's sister), called on the Vennum family to see Lurancy.

"As they came in sight, far down the street, Mary (Lurancy), looking out the window, exclaimed exultingly, 'There comes my ma and sister Nervie!' the name by which Mary used to call Mrs. Alter in childhood," Stevens wrote. "As they came into the house, she caught them around their necks, wept and cried for joy, and seemed so happy to meet them."

Lurancy's happiness at being reunited with her family was short-lived when she realized she would not be going home with them, and she grew more homesick and depressed.

A few days later the weary Vennums decided they couldn't handle the girl any longer and agreed to let her live with the Roff family.

On February 11, 1878, Lurancy arrived at the Roff house where, in Stevens's words, "she met her 'pa and ma,' and each member of the family, with the most gratifying expressions of love and affection." Lurancy told the Roffs she planned to stay with them until sometime in May.

Over the next three months and ten days, Lurancy astounded members of the Roff family, as well as their friends and relatives, with the breadth of her knowledge about things that could only have been known by Mary Roff.

For example, when a friend and former neighbor of the Roffs, Mrs. Parker, and her daughter, Nellie, came by the house, Lurancy (who had never met them before) recognized them both and asked if they could remember when she and her sister Minerva used to come to their house and sing "Mary Had A Little Lamb." Stevens noted that this would have occurred before Lurancy was born.

Another time, Asa Roff decided to test Lurancy by placing a velvet headband, beloved by Mary while she was alive, on a tea stand to see if Lurancy would recognize it. When the girl entered the room, she immediately ran to the band and said it was one that she used to wear when her hair was shorter.

"And so Mary (Lurancy) continually recognized every little thing and remembered every little incident of her girlhood," Stevens said.

During another session with Lurancy, the girl told Stevens she had seen his deceased children in heaven and described them perfectly.

On May 7 a tearful Lurancy, still channeling Mary Roff, announced to the Roff family that Lurancy would be coming back soon for good. She sat down, closed her eyes, and when she reopened them she was Lurancy.

Stevens wrote that the girl looked around the room confused and asked where she was. After she was told what had happened, she started to cry and said she wanted to go home (to the Vennums). Ann Roff said she would send for the Vennums, but Lurancy said she didn't want to wait and her personality was again submerged, replaced by Mary's spirit.

A few weeks later, on May 21, after several instances where Lurancy and Mary traded off control of Lurancy's body, Lurancy announced that Mary would be leaving for good.

But before Mary's departure, she bid her family good-bye and asked them to write to Dr. Stevens, who had returned to

Wisconsin, to tell him, "I am going to heaven, and Rancy is coming home well."

According to Stevens, who died in 1885 at the age of sixty-three, Lurancy was returned to her family, who she was overjoyed to see again. She described her experience as similar to being asleep and like living in a dream.

Remarkably Lurancy Vennum's seizures disappeared and she became, in her mother's words, "smarter, more intelligent, more industrious, more womanly, and more polite than before."

Over the next few years, Lurancy lived what might best be described as a normal, healthy life—with no reoccurrence of violent fits or other strange behavior.

According to Asa Roff, Lurancy lived happily with her parents until January 1882, when she married a local farmer named George Binning. Two years later the couple, who would have nine children, moved to Kansas and, later, to California.

Asa Roff noted that between 1878 and 1884, Lurancy would occasionally meet with his family and allow Mary to take temporary control.

"Aside from this she had little opportunity of using her mediumship, her parents being afraid to converse with her upon the subject lest it should cause a return of the 'spells' (as they called them)," he said.

With some regret Asa Roff added that after Lurancy married, her husband was not a Spiritualist, so he "furnished poor conditions for farther development in that direction."

Lurancy died on August 30, 1952, in Long Beach, California, and is buried in that city's Sunnyside Cemetery.

Not surprisingly, following the 1878 publication of Stevens's book, *The Watseka Wonder* (which sold an amazing one hundred thousand copies), there were attempts to debunk the story.

One of those who questioned its authenticity was Richard Hodgson, a renowned nineteenth-century paranormal skeptic and member of the Society for Psychical Research, which investigated psychic and spiritual phenomena.

In his 1909 book, *Historic Ghosts and Ghost Hunters,* journalist and author Henry Addington Bruce described Hodgson as "Archinquisitor of the Society for Psychical Research, the Sherlock Holmes of professional detectives of the supernatural."

According to Bruce, Hodgson traveled to Watseka in April 1890 to investigate the claim that Lurancy Vennum had channeled a woman who had been dead for twelve years (Mary Roff). He interviewed Mr. and Mrs. Roff, Minerva Alter (Mary Roff's sister), and more than a half dozen neighbors who had viewed the "possession."

He was unable to meet with Lurancy Vennum Binning because she was no longer living in Watseka. After speaking to everyone connected with the case, Hodgson reluctantly concluded that he could find nothing to discount the story.

He pronounced the case as unique in the annuals of "supernormal occurrences" and said he could not "find any satisfactory interpretation of it except the spiritistic."

Bruce, however, had his own theory of what had happened. He suggested that Lurancy Vennum had responded to subconscious cues from the Roffs and Dr. Stevens to present a version of Mary Roff that they and other family members were unconsciously projecting.

"It was necessary to tap telepathically the reservoir of information possessed by Mary's family; and there would be available besides a wealth of data in chance remarks, unconscious hints, unnoticed promptings," he wrote. "Focused thus by suggestion, that subtle, all-persuasive influence which man is only now beginning to appreciate, the basic delusional idea promptly took root, blossomed, and burst into an amazing fruition."

So, did the spirit of the dead Mary Roff really possess Lurancy Vennum for more than three months in 1878? Over the years the case has spawned a cottage industry of those who believe it's true, including more than a half dozen books, a documentary, and several cable TV shows.

The Victorian Roff House in Watseka, still standing, has been turned into a shrine to the "Watseka Wonder," complete with vintage furnishings, regularly scheduled ghost hunting expeditions, and paranormal investigation tours—even sessions with a psychic medium on New Year's Eve.

Humorist Mark Twain once wrote, "Faith is believing in something you know ain't so." In this case he probably was right.

CHAPTER 10

Invasion of the Phantom Gasbags

There was something new in the air in America in the closing years of the nineteenth century. During the decade of the 1890s, Americans saw the invention of the tabulating machine, the Ferris Wheel, the escalator, wireless radio, X-rays, the zipper, gas-powered automobiles, the mousetrap (invented in Abingdon, Illinois, in 1894), and even the game of basketball. It was a time of infinite possibilities—perhaps even machines that could fly.

Imaginative writers of the time had crafted incredible tales of fantastic scientific devices, like Jules Verne's *Twenty Thousand Leagues Under the Sea,* which featured Captain Nemo and his submarine *Nautilus,* and H. G. Wells's *Time Machine.* In nearly all of these stories, the main character was a mysterious genius inventor who created a machine that could perform amazing feats, such as travel underwater, through time, or to the moon.

Still it was a shock when, in November 1896, reports began to trickle in from Northern California about sightings of a mysterious brightly illuminated flying airship (the first untethered

111

rigid airship, the Zeppelin LZ-1, would not be tested until July 2, 1900, in Germany, and the commercial use of airships wasn't until after 1910).

The mystery ship wasn't like typical hot air balloons, which could only float along on air currents, but appeared to be a cigar-shaped navigable vessel adorned with bright spotlights.

The first sighting occurred on November 17, 1896, in the rainy and overcast skies above Sacramento, California. A small news story tucked on page four of the next day's *Sacramento Daily Record-Union* asked, "What Was It?" and reported: "Several persons last evening, between 6 and 7 o'clock saw a big ball of fire, like an electric light, pass over the city going to a southwesterly direction. It moved slowly and was in sight for more than a half-hour, finally disappearing in the mist and darkness."

The *Record-Union* story noted that several onlookers claimed to have heard human voices "engaged in song and mirth coming from above." One observer told the paper he had heard a voice warning "the man at the helm" to go higher or they would collide with a church's steeple.

The article concluded, "It is possible someone sent up an illuminated balloon, or that a stray meteor was hunting for the rest of the gang, but there really were persons who insisted that it was a newfangled airship lighted by electricity and traveling direct for San Francisco from—somewhere."

That same day, the *San Francisco Call* newspaper published a small story on page three headlined, "Claim They Saw A Flying

Airship." In the article the paper said there was considerable excitement in Sacramento after the city had been aerially buzzed by a "reputed airship."

The story said that the heavy cloud cover obscured the floating vehicle so that its shape and size were impossible to determine, but noted it had twice the brilliance of an arc light. The strange floating object, headed toward San Francisco, was said to have been about one thousand feet in the air and rose to a height of some two thousand feet.

As in the *Record-Union* story, onlookers said they heard singing voices that seemed to come from the flying thing.

By the next day the story had become front-page news. The lead story in the *San Francisco Call* was devoted to the Sacramento sightings and included an engraved drawing depicting the airship based on eyewitness accounts. The illustration showed a football-shaped balloon with four propellers and a spotlight flying over the city.

A large headline proclaimed, "Strange Craft of the Sky," while the accompanying article reported that the mysterious flying airship, which had reappeared on the evening of November 18, was the number one topic of conversation in California's capital city.

For the next week the glowing flying ship was allegedly spotted in communities throughout Northern California, including San Francisco, Oakland, and San Jose, as well as in the state of Washington and in Canada.

The busiest night for sightings was November 25, when the seemingly ubiquitous ship was spotted in eleven different communities around the state ranging from Visalia in Southern California to Chico in the far northern part of the state.

On November 23 an attorney named George D. Collins of Alameda stepped forward and told newspapers he represented the airship's inventor, who sought to remain anonymous.

According to the *Call*, Collins said a publicity-shy, forty-seven-year-old millionaire from Oroville, California, had created

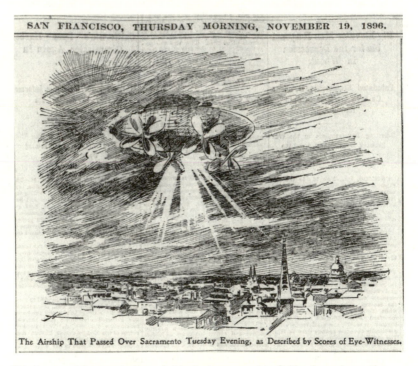

SA'N FRANCISCO, THURSDAY MORNING, NOVEMBER 19, 1896.

The Airship That Passed Over Sacramento Tuesday Evening, as Described by Scores of Eye-Witnesses.

This image of the mysterious airship that appeared in California and over the Chicago area in 1896–97 originally appeared in the *San Francisco Call,* on November 19, 1896.

the flying conveyance and was concerned someone might steal his invention, hence the secrecy.

"From what I have seen of the man and his invention," Collins told the paper, "I have no alternative but to believe implicitly all I have said."

Three days later Collins quietly relinquished his role as spokesman for the inventor (and disappeared from the debate) and was replaced by another attorney, William H. H. Hart, a former California state's attorney general.

Hart said he had been hired to replace Collins because of the latter's "loquacity" and the desire of the airship's inventor to remain anonymous.

Of course if less attention was the mystery inventor's intention, that's not what happened. Hart was even more provocative than Collins, telling newspapers there was more than one airship (on November 29 he claimed there were three) and the ultimate purpose of the flying devices would be to attack Havana, Cuba, which was involved in a popular uprising at the time.

"I'm quite convinced that two to three men could destroy the city of Havana in forty-eight hours," he told the *Call*. "From what I have seen of it I have not the least doubt but that it will carry four men and 1,000 pounds of dynamite."

By the end of November, however, the story virtually disappeared from the newspapers, at least in California. There were a few scattered sightings north of San Francisco on December 4, followed by no further activity.

However, in February and March 1897, the aerial vehicle suddenly reappeared in the skies over Nebraska, Kansas, Missouri, Michigan, and Iowa. Not surprisingly the new sightings attracted the interest of the Midwest media, including several Chicago newspapers, which began tracing the eastward movement of the airship and predicting it would arrive in the Windy City sometime in April.

Not everyone, however, was a believer. Beneath the headline, "Airship Headed For Chicago," the April 4 edition of the *Chicago Tribune* said sarcastically: "The airship which has been regaling the residents of Kansas towns must not be confounded with those aerial crafts which scientists have been trying to perfect for many years. This vessel is purely a celestial body which has taken on a few terrestrial attributes in order to accommodate itself to the limitations of human imagination."

The first sighting of the peripatetic airship in Illinois occurred on April 3, when it was spotted over Evanston.

The *Chicago Times-Herald*, which would be the most aggressive Chicago newspaper when it came to airship coverage, reported in its Sunday, April 4 edition that Kansas and Nebraska no longer had a monopoly on seeing mysterious airships.

"On the third day of April, A.D. 1897, at 8:40 p.m., a mysterious light, evidently that of an airship, was seen passing rapidly over the city, going west-northwest," the paper said. "The light was very bright, more like an electric light than anything else, and gave out a curious sort of flash at intervals."

On April 5 the illuminated object was spotted above Nashville, Illinois, located southeast of St. Louis. The *Times-Herald* reported that an unknown flying object with a large red light passed over the community at about eight o'clock in the evening.

"The fact that the object traveled from the northwest while the wind was from the southeast goes to prove it was not a balloon," the paper noted.

Two days later the flying construct was spotted over Rock Island, Illinois. According to newspaper accounts a local police officer saw a large glowing object in the sky. He described it as having a "glittering steel hull with dim wing-like fans on either side, and it swayed gently in its flight."

On April 9 the ship again passed through the Chicago area and was spotted over Evanston, Niles Center, Kankakee, and Mount Carroll.

The next day the *Times-Herald* reported: "One who was among the first to observe it says the object had all the appearance to him of being two cigar-shaped bodies attached by girders . . . A great crowd gathered near Milwaukee and Oakley Avenues and gazed at the object, trying to figure out what it might be. It was called an airship for lack of a better name."

The same day the more conservative *Chicago Tribune*, however, again mocked the sightings: "Either the long expected airship from the Pacific coast reached Chicago at 8:30 last evening or the fixed star, Alpha Orionis, shone with unusual brilliance, which was augmented by the tricks of refraction."

On April 12 the *Times-Herald* struck back with a drawing on its front page engraved from what it claimed was a genuine photograph of the object.

According to the newspaper Walter McCann, a news dealer in Rogers Park in Chicago, had snapped the photo at five thirty on the previous morning, after he saw the strange ship flying overhead. He said he had two negatives and three witnesses who could attest to seeing him shoot the images. The *Times-Herald*'s art staff examined the photos and negatives and proclaimed they had not been retouched or faked.

"The photograph is genuine and it is a mighty fine piece of photographic work at that. It would be impossible to 'fix' a negative so as to have it so perfect in the picture," the paper said. "The photograph is genuine."

Not surprisingly the *Tribune* published a story the same day headlined, "Airship Myth Yet Soars." The article said the *Tribune* had acquired a copy of the photo and taken it to its own expert who said, "It is a fake. It would impossible for a camera to take such a picture, except from a doctored photograph. In my opinion a picture was taken out in Rogers Park. Then the airship was filled in. After that a picture was taken of the prepared print."

Despite such doubts, for the next week the airship was seen flying over communities throughout Illinois including Springfield (April 11), Waukegan (April 11), Lincoln (April 12), Bloomington (April 12), Moline (April 13), Mount Vernon (April 15), Quincy (April 10 and 15), Decatur (April 16), Cairo

(April 16), Metropolis (April 17), Havana (April 20), and Rossville (April 25). On April 13 the *Springfield News* reported that an airship had actually touched down near Carlinville.

"These men saw it alight, and a man get out and fix some part of the machinery," the paper said. "They started for the place where it had alighted, but within a quarter of a mile it rose and disappeared."

Perhaps the most unusual story to appear during this time was a *Chicago Tribune* article on April 16 about a Detroit tugboat captain who claimed he had encountered a man, a woman, and a child in a "queer looking boat."

The captain said that as his tug moved closer to the trio,

A gayly [sic] decorated object was slowly inflated and rose to the length of the ropes by which it was attached to the boat.

It was a balloon, cylinder shaped, about fifty feet long. Slowly the boat rose into the air until it stood directly over the tug, about 500 feet from the water. It circled like a hawk for several minutes. Suddenly there was a splash in the water. A large sword fish had been dropped from the airship . . . and the mysterious people were carried away by the high wind.

The most famous inventor of the time, Thomas Edison, was even drawn into the airship debate when, on April 19, a letter addressed to him was reportedly dropped from an airship onto a farm near Astoria, Illinois. The letter was written in some kind of code and signed by a "C. L. Harris, electrician airship No. 3."

Reached in his New Jersey laboratory, Edison said he believed the alleged ship sightings were a hoax, although he was certain viable airships would be built in the near future. "It is absolutely absurd to imagine that a man would construct a successful airship and keep the matter secret," he said.

Still, a variety of would-be inventors and publicity seekers stepped forward to try to take credit or to say they knew those responsible for the miraculous flying ship.

In the April 10 issue of the *Chicago Tribune,* Max L. Harmar (also called Hasmar in the article), secretary of an organization calling itself the Chicago Aeronautical Society, said he was not surprised by the appearance of the airship. He said he was in contact with aviators from California who were traveling across the country. He told the newspaper:

There is only one thing that surprises me in the presence of the airship tonight. We expected it Sunday and it is hard for me to believe the vessel arrived here so soon unless the conditions were exceptionally favorable. Yes, I have a good idea concerning all this mystery. I know one of the men who is in the airship. The car contains three people, but the exaggerated stories concerning the ship are laughable.

Harmar added that the ship was not made of metal but was

constructed of paper stretched over a rigid frame. It contained "the customary inflated gas reservoir" and the big advance in its design was the fact the inventors had developed a practical method of propulsion and steering capabilities.

He said the airship would ultimately land in Washington, DC, where it would be revealed to the world. He noted that the ship had been financed by a group of wealthy individuals who preferred to remain nameless.

Two days later the *Tribune* printed a story titled, "Maker of Airship Reveals Himself," which briefly mentioned a mystery man who called himself A. C. Clinton who sent a letter to organizers of the Trans-Mississippi Exposition in Omaha, Nebraska, claiming he was the inventor of the airship. Clinton offered to display the vessel at the exposition if he was allocated thirty-five acres of space for his vehicle.

"I am the famous airship constructor and will guarantee you positively of this fact in a week," he wrote. "The airship is my own invention and as I am an Omaha man I wish it to be held as an Omaha invention."

On April 13 the *New York Times* published a short item quoting a Chicago inventor, Oscar D. Booth, as saying that he "firmly believes" Chicago had been visited by a flying airship that was built and operated by another inventor, Charles Clinton of Dodge City, Kansas.

Booth said Clinton had previously filed US patent papers

for such a flying machine, so he believed it had been constructed in Kansas and was being tested throughout the Midwest.

And yet another explanation was offered in June 1897, when Captain Joseph O'Donnell of Wilmette, Illinois, stepped forward and claimed he and an assistant had invented a fireworks machine that "sends up small balls which enlarge and become illuminated only when they have mounted to a great distance in the air."

O'Donnell said his device, which he had tested in April, was responsible for the glowing apparitions in the night sky seen by Chicagoland residents.

By May 1897 coverage of the mystery airships had ceased in most Midwestern newspapers. Even the *Times-Herald* and the *Tribune* apparently grew weary of their hissing match and stopped printing any more stories.

According to Jay Rath, author of *The I-Files: True Reports of Unexplained Phenomena in Illinois,* "After a few appearances in Indiana, the airship's eastward tour appeared to have ended."

While that's certainly true, it wasn't the last time the airship was sighted in the United States. The focus of the stories shifted south, particularly to Texas. In mid-April a handful of newspapers in the northern part of Texas began reporting sightings of the mystery aircraft.

On April 16 there were thirty-four separate sightings in communities throughout the state. In some accounts onlookers claimed they saw more than one ship in the night skies, while in others people reported meeting the ship's occupants when it landed for repairs.

On April 18 an airship allegedly crashed into a windmill and fell to the ground near Aurora, Texas. News accounts said the pilot was badly burned and his body was buried.

Some locals claimed the pilot did not appear to be human—one person said he was a man from Mars—and they had found papers on him written in some unknown language.

By May 1897 the whole affair seemed to end. Newspapers moved on to other more down-to-earth stories and there were no new reports of flying ships. So was there really an electric airship that traveled from California to the Midwest and on to Texas?

In *Solving the 1897 Airship Mystery,* published in 2004, author Michael Busby exhaustively examined all of the various newspapers' accounts—there were more than twelve hundred stories about the airship during 1896 and 1897—and found curious connections between names mentioned in some of the articles, noting that many were legitimately involved in doing research on lighter-than-air vehicles.

Busby also debunked the most popular prevailing theories, including that the sightings were the result of mass public hysteria, a secret government project that was covered up, or hoaxes perpetrated by newspapers and/or the railroad industry.

His theory? He said:

We are left to conclude that a small group of inventors and adventurers, in 1897, amazed the world for a few short days in the spring with their wonderful flying machines before unexpectedly meeting untimely ends. And perhaps locked away and forgotten in some dusty attic waiting for another helpful nurse to 'take care of that mess and clean it up' are documents that will reveal the whole airship story.

CHAPTER 11

Did Anyone Really Starve on
Starved Rock?

The year was 1769. For many years various regional Native American tribes had fought for control of the lands along the Illinois River. In this conflict the Illinois Alliance tribes, which consisted of more than a half dozen subtribes—including the Kaskaskia, Michigamea, Tamaroa, and Peoria—often clashed with the Iroquois and their allies—including the Fox and Potawatomi, which were subtribes of the Ottawa.

Additionally the Illinois tribes maintained warm relations with the French, while the Iroquois and their allies were close to the English.

The first nonnative explorers to visit the Illinois River area arrived in 1673, when an expedition led by Louis Jolliet and Jacques Marquette ascended the Illinois River and encountered a large village of the Kaskaskia tribe. Marquette later wrote that the inhabitants were friendly and "compelled me to promise to return and instruct them."

The Kaskaskia settlement was located on the north side of the Illinois River near an intriguing natural formation that later became known as Starved Rock.

A few years later another explorer, René-Robert Cavelier, Sieur de La Salle visited the area and noticed the impressive 130-foot sandstone butte that towered above the river, about a mile from the Kaskaskia village.

La Salle, who had been tasked by the King of France to establish a chain of forts to solidify France's claim on the region, immediately recognized the defensive advantages of the site, which he called *Le Rocher* ("the Rock"), and decided to build a fort atop the bluff.

Named Fort St. Louis, the battlement was completed in 1683. About a year later the fort survived its first test, an attack by the Iroquois. However, following La Salle's murder in Texas in 1687, Fort St. Louis was abandoned.

By the 1760s, the French had largely abandoned the area, which came under British control. Most of the French had retreated to the southern part of the future state of Illinois.

LIBRARY OF CONGRESS

Starved Rock, shown in this panoramic view taken in 1914, is said to have been the site of a terrible massacre in the eighteenth century.

In 1769, however, the great chief of the Ottawa people, Pontiac, was murdered, allegedly by an Illinois brave (of the Peoria or Kaskaskia tribe) while visiting Cahokia, Illinois, near St. Louis, to negotiate trade agreements with the French.

Pontiac's death incensed the Ottawa, and members of the Potawatomi and Fox tribes, bitter enemies of the Illinois, quickly set out to avenge his murder. They paddled down the Illinois River to brutally attack the Illinois village of Kaskaskia.

Following a fierce battle the surviving Illinois, said to number between one thousand and two thousand, fled to the high ground at nearby Starved Rock, which, because of its steep cliffs, would be easier to defend.

There, according to Judge John Dean Caton of Ottawa, Illinois, who authored *The Last of the Illinois and a Sketch of the Pottawatomies* [*sic*] in 1870, "they found sufficient space upon the half-acre of ground which covers the summit of Starved Rock. As its sides are perpendicular, ten men could repel ten thousand with the means of warfare then at their command."

Judge Caton based his work on interviews he conducted with an elderly Potawatomi chief named Meachelle, who said he had witnessed the attack. He said that Meachelle told him the Potawatomi decided to lay siege to the outcropping in an effort to force the Illinois to capitulate.

According to Judge Caton, the Potawatomi made no attempt to take the site but rather were content to try to starve the Illinois who were trapped on the rock. When members of the

Illinois group tried to lower containers on ropes into the Illinois River below to obtain water, the Potawatomi warriors paddled to the base of the cliff and cut their ropes.

Judge Caton reported:

At last the time came when the unfortunate remnant could hold out no longer. They awaited but a favorable opportunity to attempt their escape. This was at last afforded by a dark and stormy night, when led by their few remaining warriors, all stole in profound silence down the steep and narrow declivity to be met by a solid wall of their enemies surrounding the point where alone a sortie could be made, and which had been confidently expected.

The horrid scene that ensued can be better imagined than described.

Judge Caton wrote that the Illinois braves fell "one by one, fighting like very fiends," while the surviving women and children, "left but enfeebled skeletons," were no match for the fierce Potawatomi warriors, who clubbed them to death. "They were bent upon the utter extermination of their hated enemies," he said. "And most successfully did they bend their savage energies to the bloody task."

Judge Caton described a terrible scene: hundreds of bloody and beaten corpses of men, women, and children littered all around the rocky surface of Starved Rock. "The wails of the feeble and the strong had ceased to fret the night winds, whose mournful sighs through the neighboring pines sounded like a sad requiem," he said.

However, eleven of the most able-bodied Illinois warriors did manage to sneak through the siege lines to the river, where they found several unguarded canoes. The men quietly slipped into the dugouts and escaped down the river.

According to Judge Caton, the men knew that if they stopped to rest they would be captured by the Potawatomi—who finally noticed them and were in pursuit—so they paddled "by night and by day" until they reached St. Louis, Missouri.

Once there they fled into a military fort and begged for protection. The fort's commander turned back the Potawatomi, who eventually gave up and returned home.

Judge Caton noted:

After their enemies had gone, the Illinois, who never after even claimed that name, thanked their entertainers, and full of sorrow which no words can express, slowly paddled their way across the river to seek new friends among the tribes who then occupied the southern part of the state, and who would listen to the sad tale they had to relate. They alone remained, the broken remnant and last representatives of their once great nation . . . This is the last we know of the last of the Illinois.

Additionally, another nineteenth-century Illinois historian, Perry Armstrong, said he interviewed a second chief, an elderly

Ottawa Indian named Shick-Shack, who claimed he also was present during the tragedy.

Speaking at a pageant at Starved Rock in 1873, Armstrong recounted a tale similar to Caton's story. According to Armstrong, when the starving Illinois Indians tried to escape and encountered the waiting Potawatomi, they "were butchered and scalped. The younger squaws and the papooses were divided among the allies."

A few years later Elmer Baldwin, author of a history of La Salle County (in which Starved Rock is located) that was published in 1877, wrote that human bones could still be found scattered all about at Starved Rock.

One of the earliest mentions of the Starved Rock story showed up in a journal written by Henry Schoolcroft, who explored much of the upper Midwest, including Illinois, in the early nineteenth century.

In 1821 Schoolcroft wrote of being told a story about the death of a group of Indians at Starved Rock, which he described as a natural battlement that had been additionally fortified with "a degree of industry which the Indians have not usually bestowed upon works of defence [*sic*]."

Over time the event, known as the Starved Rock Massacre, became an accepted part of Illinois history. The easily romanticized story of the courageous but doomed Illinois hunted to near extinction by the Potawatomi appeared in dozens of books.

Perhaps the most flowery was *The Last of the Illini or The Legend of Starved Rock* by William Noble Roundy, which was published in 1916. Told in the form of an epic poem, Roundy describes a tale,

> Floated down from misty ages,
> From the twilight times long vanished.
> When the copper colored Redmen
> Roamed in pride these vast prairies,—
> Free and careless as the eagles;
> Wild as storm-clouds in a tempest;
> Happy like all things unfettered.

In his canto Roundy dramatically described the last days of the Illini, encircled atop Starved Rock without food and water:

> Many foes had flocked around them;
> Then another came unbidden,—
> Cunning as a creeping serpent;
> Silent, stealthy as a panther;—
> It was Hunger,—the fierce Demon.

He wrote of how the dying Illinois tried to survive by eating the plants and shrubs, but it wasn't enough to sustain them.

In Roundy's version of the tale, once the Illini were so weak they could not defend themselves, they were attacked by the Ottawa.

Meanwhile on the Rock's high summit,

Vengeance dire and stern was doing,

Just as if the great Chief's spirit

Had descended for a season

To inspire his friends and kinsmen:

Raising high their red stone axes;

Lifting up their bloody daggers, . . .

In the darkened twilight shadows,

Far above the placid river,

This victorious song was chanted;—

Thus was Pontiac's death atoned for.

In 1911 the state of Illinois purchased Starved Rock and the surrounding 280 acres for $146,000 to use as a public park. One of the park's biggest proponents was William Osman Jr., longtime editor of the *Ottawa Free Trader* newspaper, who, with a friend, attorney Horace Hull of Ottawa, traveled around the state promoting the idea.

Not coincidentally, in 1895, Osman's son, Eaton, authored a popular history of Starved Rock that prominently featured the story of the massacre.

But is it a true story? Illinois historian Mark Walczynski, who has studied dozens of accounts of the event, has uncovered inconsistencies that have made him wonder if the legendary Starved Rock Massacre ever took place.

In an article that appeared in the *Journal of the Illinois State Historical Society* in 2007, Walczynski wrote that despite the fact that more than a half dozen formal archaeological surveys and excavations have been conducted on and around Starved Rock over the years, "no evidence of a large massacre, battle, or siege that occurred in 1769 has been found.

"No evidence of genocide was found on the summit of the Rock, at the base of the Rock, or anywhere near the Rock. The silence in the reports is deafening. Despite extensive study and excavation, there is no physical evidence of a massacre at Starved Rock."

Additionally, Walczynski noted that some of the basic elements of the Starved Rock story didn't make sense. He wondered why the Illinois, allegedly dying of thirst, decided to slip away during a thunderstorm rather than collect rainwater and try to regain their strength before mounting an escape effort.

He also questioned how the eleven surviving warriors, who, presumably, were also weakened and dying of hunger and thirst, could paddle canoes through the Illinois River rapids at night and continue nonstop for more than two hundred miles to St. Louis.

And why, he asked, have modern-day archaeologists found no human bones or other evidence of a massacre, siege, or battle?

Walczynski, however, does believe something happened on Starved Rock. His research has led him to conclude that the stories surrounding what happened at Starved Rock most likely can be traced to a much earlier attack at the same location.

According to Walczynski, the precursor event occurred in 1722, when a group of Fox warriors trapped a group of Peoria tribe members atop Starved Rock. The Fox hostilities against the Peoria came during the so-called Fox Wars, when the French and their allies, including the Illinois tribes, clashed with the Fox in a series of turf battles between 1712 and 1730.

Apparently in 1721 a party of Fox warriors attacked the French community of Kaskaskia in Southern Illinois, killing a number of Illinois along with a French soldier. A war party that included French soldiers and Illinois warriors quickly set out after the Fox.

They eventually captured more than two dozen of them, including Minchilay, a nephew of a prominent Fox chief named Ouashala. The prisoners were turned over to the Illinois, who decided to send a message by burning all the captives to death.

Not surprisingly, Ouashala demanded retribution for his nephew's death and ordered his Fox warriors to attack and destroy the Peoria village at Starved Rock. The following year a large Fox war party descended on the unsuspecting villagers, many of whom fled to the top of Starved Rock.

"It is likely that the non-combatants climbed to the summit of the Rock and were later joined by the defending warriors," Walczynski wrote. "The Peoria were [then] besieged on top of Starved Rock by the Fox war-party."

Ouashala later told a French missionary that his fighters surrounded the Rock and after some time the Peoria were beginning to die of hunger and thirst. Ouashala said they requested a "parley," meaning they wanted to discuss the terms of their surrender.

Despite opposition from some of his more bloodthirsty warriors who had no interest in negotiating and wanted to slaughter the Peorians, Ouashala prevailed on his men to accept the surrender of the Peoria and spare their lives. He said to do so would be a good faith gesture because the French governor of Canada, Pierre François de Rigaud, Marquis de Vaudreuil, had once spared the lives of the Fox during a similar siege.

"Eventually the warriors, with much apprehension, acquiesced to their leader's decision," Walczynski said. "The Fox warparty left the Rock and headed for home."

Unlike the alleged massacre of 1769—which is largely supported by anecdotal evidence—the 1722 event was mentioned in several authoritative sources of the time, including a 1723 report from the Marquis de Vaudreuil to his French superiors and an earlier report from the inspector general of Louisiana (at the time a French colony) stating that he had sent a force of forty French soldiers and some four hundred Illinois to Starved Rock to provide assistance to the besieged Peoria tribe at Starved Rock.

Walczynski said that as a direct result of the 1722 siege, the Illinois withdrew from the Upper Illinois Valley, including the area around Starved Rock. In the 1730s, after the end of hostilities with the Fox (at least for awhile), the Illinois gradually began to migrate back to their former haunts along the Illinois River.

"What is known is that the Peoria sub-tribe of the Illinois Alliance was besieged by the Fox Indians in 1722 resulting in a negotiated truce," Walczynski concluded. "This real and verifiable historical event is, with little doubt, the origin of the Starved Rock Legend."

CHAPTER 12

The New Monster of the Midway

August 22, 2011, was hot and humid—a typical summer day in Chicago. The air was heavy and the sky was cloudy with patches of blue. A man and his wife—they declined to be named—stopped on the corner of 63rd Street and Pulaski Road to shoot a photo of a Windy City landmark, the giant statue of an Indian wearing glasses (it promotes a local optometrist's office), that stands atop a building. The man pulled out his smartphone and took four photos. He later wrote on a MUFON (Mutual Unidentified Flying Object Network) website:

> So we left and went home and later on that night I went to look at the pictures I took. When I was checking these photos out, in one of the pictures I notice the object that was on the backside of the Indian. At first I didn't think nothing of it—I figured it was a plane or something.

But just for the heck of it I enlarged it. It looked something similar to a bird or a bat, but then again it doesn't. So I have no idea what it could be. I was reluctant to send it in because I figured there was explanation for what it is. But then I thought it still qualifies as a UFO, because I have never seen anything like it before.

What did the couple see? A close examination of the photos reveals a fuzzy image of what appears to be some kind of black and red, winged human-shaped object floating in the sky behind the giant Indian statue. A hoax? The man insisted the photo was unretouched or changed in any way.

About a month later, on September 30, 2011, there was a report of two young women who lived near the University of Illinois at Chicago being frightened by a giant winged creature peering into their apartment, which was located on the third floor of a five-story building. The women described the figure as having glowing orange or red eyes. The women said that others had also seen the batlike thing in a park across the street from the apartment.

One of the women said that her boyfriend and his best friend saw the creature and,

It was perched on top of a basketball hoop in the neighborhood park . . . it saw them and had alighted into the air with an audible whoosh. He [the boyfriend] states that there were about 6 people in the park and all of them had seen it when it had taken off. He states there was no way anyone could have missed it, it was about 6–7 feet tall, dark grey to black and those eyes glowed with the intensity of two glowing embers.

On October 14, there was yet another sighting of the mysterious flying phantom. This time the eyewitness was a University of Illinois at Chicago student who was walking through a community park near the campus with his girlfriend.

The student said,

It looked like a man, it looked like a man with wings! He flew about 10–12 feet above us and was perfectly silhouetted against the evening sky. In all honesty, it looked like an immensely oversized Sugar Glider [a small gliding possum native to Australia and Tasmania], the kind I would see back home in Tasmania. It had the rough shape of a sugar glider, but its eyes were nothing like the soft eyes of a glider. They glowed red!

So what was it? According to a number of UFO and paranormal websites, the flying creature was no less than the return of the Mothman, a mysterious harbinger of doom that reportedly originally appeared in West Virginia in the mid-1960s. In the words of one site, www.meetstheweird.com, "It looks as if a Mothman may have paid a visit to the Windy City."

The original Mothman has been the subject of a handful of books and documentaries as well as a 2002 movie, *The Mothman*

Prophecies, which starred Richard Gere and Laura Linney. The first reported sighting of Mothman was near Point Pleasant, West Virginia, in mid-November 1966.

"Two Point Pleasant couples said today they encountered a man-sized, bird-like creature in the TNT area [a wildlife refuge located on the former site of an ammunition plant] about midnight last night," reported the *Point Pleasant Register* on November 16. "The two young men telling their story this morning were dead serious, and asserted they hadn't been drinking."

According to the article Steve Mallette and Roger Scarberry and their wives were sitting in Scarberry's car between eleven thirty and midnight when they saw the winged creature. "It was like a man with wings," Mallette said. "It wasn't like anything you'd ever see on TV or in a monster movie."

The men said the birdman had a clumsy gait when it walked on the ground but was extremely fast and agile when in the air. Scarberry said that after the two couples spotted the thing they grew scared and decided to drive away as quickly as they could. However, the monster rose into the air like a helicopter and followed them, easily keeping pace. He said it finally flew off after the car reached town.

"It apparently is afraid of light," Mallette told the paper. "And maybe it thought it was scaring us off."

The two men described the creature as being gray or brown in color, six feet tall, with a ten-foot wingspan and glowing red eyes.

The following day, under the tongue-in-cheek headline, "City Getting 'The Bird,' Want it or Not," the *Register's* editor, John Samsell, reported that other local residents had also encountered the strange winged being.

According to Samsell, four local youths claimed something looking like a "huge bird" came around their car, stared at them, and flew off. Sheriff George Johnson said the four young people clearly had "seen something unusual to scare them." He hypothesized, however, that it was most likely an oversize crane or some other bird.

Two days later the United Press International (UPI) wire service reported that as many as eight people in central and northern West Virginia had seen some kind of flying creature in recent days. One of those people was Kenneth Duncan of Blue Creek, West Virginia, who was digging his brother-in-law's grave with several other men when "something that 'looked like a brown human being' buzzed past."

Duncan described the flying thing as having large crimson eyes that shined like "red reflectors" and a wingspan of about ten feet.

Another man, Newell Partridge, said he had seen some kind of flying creature near his home, located about one hundred miles north of Point Pleasant, about ninety minutes before Duncan's sighting. He said it began when his television set "began acting like a generator" and his German shepherd, Bandit, started "carrying on something terrible."

When he went outside to see what was causing the com-motion, he spotted something with shiny red eyes in his field. Before he could stop his dog, it ran barking into the field toward the bizarre creature. He never saw the dog again.

The UPI story quoted local law enforcement officials as believing the creature was a "freak shitepoke," an unusually large member of the heron family of birds. "Officials were at a loss, however, to explain how a shag [shitepoke] could fly at 100 miles per hour," the story concluded.

As the stories spread beyond West Virginia, other newspa-pers coined new names for the mysterious flying creature. One Midwest editor apparently decided to name it after one of the villains—"Killer Moth"—from the then-popular *Batman* TV show. Thus "Mothman" was born.

The attention attracted crowds of people to Point Pleasant, including John A. Keel, an American journalist who specialized in UFO stories and the supernatural. In the months following the first Mothman sightings, Keel interviewed dozens of West Virginians who claimed to have seen the creature. His subse-quent book, *The Mothman Prophecies,* was the basis for the Richard Gere film.

According to Keel, the Mothman was most likely extrater-restrial in origin and possibly related to UFO sightings made in the same part of the country that same year.

In his book Keel wrote that some people received warnings, usually via strange telephone calls, that something bad was about

In 2011, the mysterious figure called Mothman—said to be a harbinger of bad things—was allegedly seen flying over Chicago's Pulaski Street neighborhood. Note: This photograph has been manipulated to reflect what a witness alleges to have seen.

to happen, but neither he nor they understood how to interpret the messages.

"Something unnatural was stalking the hills of West Virginia that November," he wrote. "The fear would become contagious."

Keel estimated that during a thirteen-month period between 1966 and 1967, more than one hundred people said they had some kind of encounter with the Mothman. He wrote:

> Everyone was now seeing Mothman or the 'Bird,' or so it seemed. Sightings were reported in Mason, Lincoln, Logan, Kanawha, and Nicholas counties. People were traveling for hundreds of miles to sit in the cold TNT area all night, hoping to glimpse the creature. Those who were unlucky enough to see it vowed they never wanted to see it again. It evoked unspeakable terrors.
>
> Like flying saucers, it delighted in chasing cars . . . a very unbirdlike habit, and it seemed to have a penchant for scaring females who were menstruating, another UFO/hairy monster peculiarity.

The Mothman appearances finally stopped on December 15, 1967, according to Keel. That was the day the Silver Bridge collapsed, killing forty-six people and severely injuring nine others.

The Silver Bridge (named for the color of its aluminum paint) was a high-tension, eyebar-chain suspension span constructed in 1928. It crossed over the Ohio River, linking Point Pleasant, West Virginia, to Kanauga, Ohio, and it was one of the major routes between the two states.

The official reason for the bridge's collapse was that it had failed because of a defect in a single link that, over time, caused stress-corrosion cracking. At the time it collapsed, the bridge was carrying thirty-seven cars; thirty-one of those fell into the river.

"I'd had warnings about something terrible that was going to happen," Keel wrote. "If I could have put things together sooner, maybe we could have saved all those lives."

Of course since Mothman's previous appearances have always seemed to foreshadow some kind of disaster, what was he possibly saying with his recent visits to Chicago? According to the website www.meetstheweird.com, on Friday, October 8, shortly after the first two sightings in Chicago, a train derailed and caught fire near Elgin, located about thirty-four miles northwest of the city. The site administrator wrote:

I can't believe that I failed to make the connection. The derailment set off a series of massive explosions that caused the evacuation of the 800 residents of the small town of Tiskilwa, Illinois. Amazingly, no one was hurt in the accident.

Could the Mothman sighting be linked to this accident, or is something else in store for Chicago?

Stay tuned.

CHAPTER 13

Virgil Ball's Obsession

For nearly a half century, Virgil Ball was absolutely certain he knew what had happened to Fay Rawley. He just couldn't prove it.

On November 8, 1953, Rawley, a fifty-six-year-old, well-to-do farmer from the small west-central Illinois hamlet of Summum and a Fulton County supervisor, along with his 1953 green, four-door Cadillac sedan, disappeared without a trace. Some claimed he ran away—although no one could ever say why he might do so—while others insisted he was murdered.

At the time, Ball was the deputy sheriff of Fulton County (he would also serve a term as sheriff from 1954 to 1958 and was later elected Fulton County treasurer), and he was tasked with finding out what happened to Rawley. By most accounts Rawley was well liked and a charitable man—he was said to have been lenient and understanding when collecting on his rental properties—but also had a reputation as a ladies' man. In fact the day after his disappearance, Rawley, who had been separated from his wife for more than seven years, was scheduled to finalize his divorce.

The last person to see Rawley was Mrs. Helen Wagner of Macomb, Illinois, a recent divorcee he had been dating. On the night of November 8, when Rawley had visited her, she told him she was breaking off their relationship and returning to her ex-husband.

Mrs. Wagner later told police that Rawley was understandably upset but otherwise fine when he drove off in his green Cadillac for the fifty-mile return trip to Summum.

Ball, who died in 1999 at the age of eighty-five, was so convinced that Rawley was the victim of foul play that he became nearly obsessed with the case. Described as stubborn and determined, Ball had been a Marine Raider during World War II and, after being injured, had spent nine months in rehabilitation hospitals.

"My father never, ever, ever gave up on something," noted his son, John, in a *Peoria Journal-Star* article shortly after his death. "He didn't know how to quit. He believed that the evidence that he had developed definitely pointed to that mine being the location of Mr. Rawley's body."

The mine in question was the Peabody Corporation's Key Mine, a massive coal strip mine located adjacent to Rawley's farm. A few years after Rawley had disappeared, Ball had received a tip that the missing man and his vehicle were buried somewhere in the mine.

In 1957 Ball organized a formal excavation of the mine. On April 24, 1955, the *Chicago Tribune* noted:

Fulton County Sheriff Virgil Paul [*sic*] said today he has called upon science for aid in solving the disappearance 17 months ago of a wealthy landowner he believes was murdered and buried with his new Cadillac automobile in a coal strip mine. The sheriff said he hopes to solve the mystery through computations now being made by Professor M. B. Buell of the University of Illinois based on operation by the professor of an instrument described as a magnetometer.

According to the *Tribune,* earlier that week Buell had visited the mine site and taken readings with his magnetometer, a device that was said to be capable of locating buried metal.

The article said the sheriff had received confidential information indicating that Rawley and his car were "buried in the desolate area of lakes and ridges of raw earth."

The *Tribune* reported that Ball believed "the slayers left the car, with the body inside, in a place where it might have been covered by a shovel without having been seen by the shovel's operator."

It was two years before Ball could gather the resources to begin a physical search for Rawley. In late July 1957 he supervised a crew of mine workmen who started excavating the bottom of a sixty-foot-deep abandoned strip mine using a power shovel.

The work soon attracted dozens of spectators, who lined the pit in anticipation of seeing the crews pull a green Cadillac from its depths. Ball told a United Press International (UPI) reporter that he believed Rawley had been stuffed into the trunk of his car and the car was dumped into the mine pit, which was subsequently filled with mine waste.

Unfortunately, as the work crew began digging into the pit, it filled with water, which slowed down the search.

"While pumps drained away the water, men prodded at the bottom of the pit with steel poles and said they struck something that sounded like metal," noted an August 2, 1957, UPI story.

In a clear indication of Ball's bulldogged commitment to solving the crime, the story said Ball would be having the crew "back on the job" after dinner in order to avoid the crowds that "hovered at the rim of the crater."

The workmen, however, were forced to quit digging after the sides of the pit collapsed later that same day.

"Sheriff Virgil Ball narrowly missed being trapped by the cave-in Friday," noted UPI. "He saw the avalanche of earth in time to race out of the bottom of the excavation."

In the article, Ball said tons of dirt had reburied "a piece of metal he'd hoped would provide a major clue in Rawley's disappearance. He described the metal as about 10 inches in diameter, shiny and chrome-like in appearance."

Ball told the press he believed the metal scrap was part of Rawley's car. He indicated digging would resume the following week.

Mining officials, however, were starting to wonder whether the sheriff's theory was right. On August 7, 1957, mining officials, who had provided the work crews and equipment to dig for Rawley and his car, said they would allow Ball one more day to prove his case.

"Assistant Mine Superintendent Ual Simler said that if the tests with the magnetometer do not show conclusively the car is present, the company will order the power shovel off the job," reported UPI. A dragline scoop (a type of large shovel pulled by cables) dug a 150-foot gash in the mine site, but nothing was found and the search was discontinued.

But Ball wasn't ready to give up. In July 1962 he mounted a second effort, partly funded out of his own pocket, to once again search for Rawley at the Key Mine site. The second dig generated even more public attention, attracting reporters from *Life* and *Look* magazines.

Local newspapers printed photographs showing a field jammed with automobiles and crowds outside of the pit area, as well as a solid line of onlookers standing on the rim of a massive chasm, watching the excavation. Other photos depicted workmen prodding the watery depths of the pit with long metal poles, as well as a dragline scoop being pulled through the mud.

A *Peoria Journal-Star* graphic detailed Ball's hypothesis about what had happened to Rawley. It depicted a small car in the bottom of a pit with a dragline scoop dumping dirt atop of it. A caption noted: "Sheriff Ball's theory is outlined in this sketch. He believes the drag-line operator, despite a glaring searchlight, would not have seen a car enter the strip mine because of a 20-foot shelf between him and the road where the car is parked."

In the July 20, 1962, issue of the *Journal-Star*, reporter Bernadine Martin wrote that four bulldozers were being used

RICHARD MORENO COLLECTION

Fay Rawley, a prominent central Illinois farmer and politician, who, along with his green Cadillac, mysteriously disappeared in 1953.

to push away the dirt on a part of the mine where Ball believed Rawley and his vehicle were buried. Martin reported:

> Virgil Ball, Fulton County Treasurer and former sheriff, said he still expected that it would be late tomorrow or Sunday before the crucial 43-foot depth is reached. At 45 feet or thereabouts Ball will find out whether Rawley, a wealthy Summum farmer and landowner who disappeared in 1953, is buried in his Cadillac in an abandoned strip mine. Ball thinks Rawley, 56, when he vanished, was murdered.

Not surprisingly, Ball incorporated any potentially useful method and technology—old and new—in the search.

In addition to having workers walk the site with electronic metal detectors, he recruited several "water witches"—a traditional way of finding underground water using a Y-shaped wooden branch—to help find Rawley's car.

"Water witching was tried for the first time by Bill Imlay, superintendent of the Peabody Coal Co. Key mine at Summum yesterday in an effort to locate water used in lubricating drilling operations during exploration tests for Fay Rawley's car," noted the *Journal-Star*. "Using a peach twig, Imlay apparently located water when the twig dipped violently."

As before, the quest attracted plenty of attention. The *Journal-Star* even printed the lyrics to a song written by a Springfield teenager, Frank Cellini, which was titled, "The Ballad of Fay Rawley" as well as a poem, "Ode to Virgil Ball." A theme in both was the resolute Sheriff Virgil Ball bravely carrying on the search for the missing Rawley in spite of his detractors.

Following several weeks of searching with nothing to show, the effort was abruptly called off. In a 1998 article that appeared in the *Zephyr* weekly newspaper of Galesburg, Illinois, Ball's friend, Charlie Parkinson, wrote, "As time passed, so did the interest and the crowds. However, the (Fulton) County Board was in the process of hearing from disgruntled Fulton County taxpayers who made it known they had had enough, expensewise, in regards to the search."

According to Parkinson, however, the effort ended abruptly after one of the drills had encountered something hard in the ground.

"Suddenly the word was out that they had indeed came across a vast mass of metal that could very well be the automobile and perhaps the body of Rawley," Parkinson wrote. "Suddenly, as quickly as it started, the operation ceased there at the digging site."

Parkinson said Ball was told by mining company officials that its lawyers had informed them they could be sued if Rawley and his vehicle were unearthed, so they called off the search.

"Thus ended what was perhaps the greatest manhunt in Fulton County history," Parkinson said. "Closing forever, or so it seems, what was one man's attempt to see justice done here on the plains of the Prairie State."

So what could have happened to Fay Rawley on the night of November 8, 1953?

At the time of his disappearance, Rawley was a successful farmer, landlord, and well-liked local politician. He was fifty-six years old and five feet, eight inches tall, weighing 175 pounds. He had blue eyes and dark hair and was partially bald. He wore a hearing aid on his left ear and had false teeth. He reportedly walked with a slight limp and swung his left hand when he walked. He was obtaining a divorce from his wife, Hazel, allegedly because of his marital indiscretions, and had a son, Robert, who was twenty-nine years old at the time of the disappearance.

In the early evening of November 8, Rawley had driven from his home in Summum to Macomb to see Mrs. Helen Wagner, an attractive forty-one-year-old divorcee and former neighbor, who he had been dating. Rawley apparently wanted to talk to her about getting more serious, but she told him she had decided to return to her former husband, Theodore. At eight ten that evening, Rawley said good-bye to Wagner, drove off in his green Cadillac, presumably to return home to Summum, and was never seen again.

Since Rawley was estranged from his wife and lived alone, his disappearance wasn't noticed for about two weeks. Parkinson said that employees of the mining property across the street from Rawley's home had noticed that the porch light had been on continuously for a number of days and nights, but didn't think to investigate.

When the authorities were finally alerted some fourteen days later, they entered Rawley's house and found what Parkinson later described as "a home that gave evidence of perhaps a minor skirmish taking place quite rapidly, in what could have been, earlier, a tranquil evening by its owner. Rawley's eyeglasses lay on the floor near his chair and a floor lamp was still on. His pants lay on the floor near the chair. Rawley was nowhere to be seen and his 1953 green Cadillac was not on the premises."

Lawman Ball began an immediate investigation but found few leads. Rawley's financial holdings were untouched and nothing had been taken from his home.

In the months following the disappearance, Robert Rawley posted a $2,000 reward for information leading to the whereabouts of his missing father. Sadly, on March 14, 1961, Robert Rawley died in a tragic automobile accident on Route 9, north of Cuba.

Ball conducted interviews with anyone connected to Rawley, including former lovers, their potentially disgruntled boyfriends and husbands, people who owed him money, and even those who might have had a political beef with him, but he came up empty.

According to Parkinson, Ball finally found someone who said that a car resembling Rawley's distinctive Cadillac had been seen on the evening prior to the disappearance in the mining property across from Rawley's home.

"It was then theorized by the Sheriff, that Rawley could have been taken from his home, placed in his Cadillac, driven to the mine, and covered forever," Parkinson wrote. This tip led to Ball's search of the mine area, which would continue on and off for the next five years.

After the sudden end to the 1962 excavation, Ball moved on to other things but always had the Rawley disappearance in the back of his mind. (Rawley was declared legally dead on November 8, 1960, exactly seven years after his disappearance.)

In a 1984 *Journal-Star* article, Ball said he had no regrets about all the effort he had put into trying to find Rawley and his car.

"Damn, I'd do it again in a second," he said. "The car is there, just another 15, 20 feet; that's all. Hey, with the proper equipment, I (once) offered to bet a guy my wife, my car, my house . . . You think he took it?"

In that interview, Ball said he knew who committed the crime but couldn't do anything about it without evidence.

"One of 'em is still out there," he said but noted that his primary suspect had died. As to their identities, that was information Ball would take to the grave.

"He wished to hell he could have solved it," Parkinson told the *Journal-Star* following Ball's death. "He swore he had it in the palm of his hand."

So what happened to Fay Rawley? Neither he nor his green Cadillac has resurfaced in the six decades since his disappearance.

Some, like Sheriff Ball, believed a pair of individuals probably attacked Rawley in his home, tucked his body into the trunk of his car, and drove the vehicle to the nearby strip mine where an unsuspecting shovel operator buried it under tons of dirt.

As for a motive, his home showed signs of a struggle, but police determined nothing had been stolen. While Ball never revealed his theory, many believe Rawley—who was, after all, a bit of a player—was the victim of a jealous husband or boyfriend, or a jilted lover.

Or maybe Rawley, newly dumped by his girlfriend, just climbed into his Cadillac, gunned the engine, and drove off into oblivion. Stranger things have happened.

CHAPTER 14

The Diabolical Dr. Holmes

Chicago has had its share of people who embrace their darker impulses but perhaps none as depraved as Herman Webster Mudgett—better known by his alias, Dr. Henry Howard Holmes—who was one of America's first documented serial killers.

Between 1886 and 1894, Holmes is believed to have murdered between nine and two hundred people. Some of his victims were young women who came to the city to find work during the 1893 Chicago World's Fair. Holmes coaxed them into lodging in his "murder" hotel that he specially built to conceal his crimes.

In addition to not knowing exactly how many people Holmes killed—he claimed different numbers at different times, and even police were unsure—the biggest mystery surrounding the good doctor is why did he do it?

In a "confession" that appeared in the *Philadelphia North American* newspaper on April 11, 1896, he offered one possible explanation: "Yes I was born with the devil in me . . . I was born with the evil one standing as my sponsor beside the bed where I was ushered into the world, and he has been with me since." He admitted to killing twenty-seven people but said he could not help himself.

He wrote:

> The inclination to murder came to me as naturally as the inspiration to do right comes to the majority of persons. I was not satisfied in taking it [life] in the ordinary way. I sought devices strange, fantastical and even grotesque. It pleased my fancy. It gave me play to work my murderous will, and I reveled in it with the enthusiasm of an alchemist who is hot on the trail of the philosopher's stone.

Holmes's statement to the *North American,* however, wasn't the only official confession he would make. He also sold, for a reported $7,500, his "exclusive" story to two other newspapers, including the rival *Philadelphia Inquirer* and the *New York Morning News.*

Interestingly, each confession was slightly different from the next, with the *North American* version being the most dramatic and explicit. For example, only the *North American* confession contained Holmes's eerie statement about being born with the devil inside of him.

Many experts believe the *North American* obtained an advance copy of the *Inquirer* confession and decided to enhance the account to make it more sensational.

Erik Larson, author of *The Devil in the White City,* a

best-selling historical nonfiction book that interweaves Holmes's murder spree and the 1893 Chicago World's Fair, told *C-Span Book Notes* host Brian Lamb in 2003 (when the book was published) that he believed Holmes was a classic example of a psychopath. Larson said:

> A true psychopath of this character is a guy who simply has no moral core. He doesn't have to think about being evil. He does not have to contrive to being evil. It's just what he does. And when you're like that, it's a very powerful position to be in, because you can do anything. And that's why he got

HERMAN WEBSTER MUDGETT *alias* H. H. HOLMES.

Mug shot of H. H. Holmes.

CHICAGO HISTORY MUSEUM (ICHi-27826)

away with it. You can convince anyone of anything, because you don't have that sort of moral break that allows people to detect deception.

But what in Holmes's background could have pushed him to become a serial killer? Born on May 16, 1861, in Gilmanton, New Hampshire, Holmes described himself as an ordinary country boy who didn't give his good, God-fearing parents (Levi and Theodate Mudgett) much trouble.

However, in *The Devil in the White City,* Larson wrote that Holmes's parents were devout Methodists who believed in corporal punishment for routine offenses, so it was likely he was familiar with the rod. He said some observers also suggested that young Holmes indulged in the live dismembering of small animals.

In an autobiographical booklet titled, *Holmes' Own Story,* which he published in 1895 while in a Pennsylvania jail awaiting his fate, the doctor recounted an event that had made a lasting impression on him. He said that when he walked home from school every day he passed the local doctor's office, a place that scared him.

One day two classmates learned of his fear and dragged him inside. There, he was thrust face-to-face with "one of its grinning skeletons, which with arms outstretched, seemed ready in its turn to seize me."

Holmes wrote that the experience traumatized him, but in a

good way—"it proved an heroic method of treatment" that instilled a curiosity about medicine and the desire to become a doctor.

Not surprisingly the rest of the document is a self-serving attempt to proclaim his innocence and lay blame for the murders of some of his alleged victims on a woman, Minnie Williams, and a mysterious man that he called "Hatch" (it would later be revealed that Holmes had killed Williams some time earlier and that Hatch did not exist).

He protested that he was incapable of the horrible crimes he had been accused of committing and concluded, "I feel justified in asking from the general public a suspension of judgment as to my guilt or innocence, not while the various charges can be proven against me, but while I can disprove them, a task which I feel able to satisfactorily and expeditiously accomplish."

A bright and personable young man, Holmes graduated from high school at the age of sixteen and was enrolled in the University of Vermont for about a year before transferring to the University of Michigan Medical School in Ann Arbor.

In 1878 Holmes—seemingly on the pathway to becoming a respectable doctor—married Clara A. Lovering of Alton, New Hampshire, daughter of a well-to-do New England family.

However, all was not as it seemed. Shortly after graduating from the University of Michigan, Holmes concocted a scheme involving stealing cadavers from the medical school anatomy laboratory, disfiguring the bodies so as to be virtually unidentifiable, and then staging an accident and claiming the insurance money. While the plan was never carried to fruition, it planted the seeds for Holmes's future plans.

In August 1884 Holmes arrived in Chicago, where he quickly ingratiated himself with the wife of an ailing pharmacist, E. S. Holton, who owned a drugstore on the corner of Wallace and 63rd Streets in a neighborhood on the city's south side called Englewood.

Impressed by his charm as well as his medical background, Mrs. Holton hired Holmes to help her with the pharmacy. Soon, the affable Holmes had taken over most of the operation, including maintaining the business ledgers, which allowed Mrs. Holton to spend more time with her husband, who was dying of cancer.

After Mr. Holton died, Holmes agreed to purchase the drugstore from his widow. The terms of the sale were that Holmes would pay her $100 per month and permit her to live in her quarters on the second floor of the building.

Within a short time, however, customers noticed that Mrs. Holton was no longer around. When asked about her, Holmes said she had gone to California to visit relatives and, later, that she had liked it so much she had decided relocate there. She was never seen again.

Holmes did well with the business and in 1887 married Myrta Belnap, an attractive, young blonde woman he had met during a brief stay in Minneapolis—despite the fact he was still married (as Herman Mudgett) to Clara Lovering, who was living in New Hampshire. Myrta soon gave birth to a daughter,

Lucy. There were, however, strains in the marriage. According to Larson, Holmes was a handsome, confident young man with striking blue eyes, who often flirted with his customers, many of whom seemed to be attractive young women.

Myrta relocated to Wilmette, on Chicago's north side, to live closer to her parents. Despite their separation, Holmes apparently visited semi-regularly and was described by Myrta as an attentive father and husband.

In the summer of 1888, Holmes purchased an undeveloped plot of land across the street from the drugstore. He began drawing plans for a commercial building that would have shops on the first floor and rented rooms on two upper floors.

But this building wasn't a typical retail-hotel structure. Holmes incorporated a number of unusual features, including a secret wooden chute from the second floor to the basement; a hidden walk-in, airtight vault with a gas jet he could control from his second-floor office; a variety of secret rooms without windows; and a large basement furnace.

To keep construction crews from knowing exactly what they were building—and to save money—he concocted a scheme by which he would hire day-labor carpenters to work on some aspect of the structure, accuse them of shoddy workmanship, and then fire them while refusing to pay them. This meant that no one was ever able to get a comprehensive picture of the whole project, and he could build it at a fraction of what it should have cost.

When construction was completed in 1890, Holmes's

hotel boasted five retail shops, including Holmes's new drugstore operation (he sold the former Holton store) on the first floor and a bizarre maze of rooms on the upper two levels.

The second floor had six corridors with thirty-five rooms, while the third floor had another thirty-six rooms. Because of its rounded exterior windows, people in the neighborhood began referring to it as "the castle."

It's not known how many people were lured into Holmes's castle only to disappear. After it was announced that Chicago would host the 1893 World's Fair, Holmes began marketing his property to fair visitors.

Investigators believe that among his first victims in the new hotel were Julia Conner and her eight-year-old daughter, Pearl. In 1891 the two arrived in Chicago with Julia's husband, Ned, and her sister, Gertrude. Ned took a job at the jewelry counter inside of Holmes's drugstore, and the family moved into an apartment on the second floor, adjacent to Holmes's quarters.

Ned Conner soon began to suspect his wife was having an affair with Holmes. Following months of growing ever more distant from his wife, he finally left her and filed for a divorce.

Larson noted that once Julia was no longer married, Holmes seemed to lose interest in her. After she became pregnant and demanded he marry her, Julia gave into Holmes's powers of persuasion and allowed him to perform an abortion.

In his *Inquirer* confession, Holmes claimed she died during the operation and he disposed of her body. Always the humanitarian, he said he then poisoned Pearl to spare the little girl from the pain of losing her mother and to keep her from being tossed into the city's foster care system.

While there were no doubt others who came into Holmes's murderous orbit, his next known victim was Emeline Cigrand, a twenty-four-year-old blonde stenographer who came to work for the doctor and was soon seduced by his charms.

While Cigrand was initially infatuated with the seemingly sophisticated physician, she apparently began to notice that things were not as they seemed with Holmes. He seemed to be successful yet was always being harassed by creditors, and his hotel was just plain *strange*.

In early December 1892 Cigrand hinted to friends that she might leave Holmes. A few days later she disappeared. When Holmes was asked about her, he said she had gone away to be married and produced a wedding announcement. In his confession Holmes acknowledged that he had tricked Cigrand into his vault room, where he gassed her to death.

In 1893 Holmes reacquainted himself with Minnie Williams, whom he had met earlier during business trips to Boston. He had courted Minnie, a dowdy woman in her late twenties, but dropped her when his visits became less frequent. When he found she had relocated to Chicago, he hired her as his personal secretary.

As with his other victims, Holmes asked her to marry him

and then persuaded her to turn over ownership of valuable property she had inherited in Texas to an associate of his to develop (the associate, naturally, was simply another of Holmes's pseudonyms).

Shortly after, Holmes and Williams were wed before a preacher—although it was probably a fake ceremony since no record of the marriage was ever formally filed.

In June 1893 Minnie Williams's younger sister, Anna, visited Chicago for the first time. Holmes invited her to stay with him and her sister and took her to tour the castle. Once there, however, Holmes took her into the vault room, where he asphyxiated her. He then poisoned Minnie Williams and buried her body in the basement of a house he had rented in another part of the city.

In his confession Holmes said he had killed both of them because they were no longer needed after he had acquired their money and property.

During the construction of the castle, one of the men hired by Holmes was a carpenter named Benjamin Pietzel, who eventually became his accomplice on various fraudulent financial transactions. An alcoholic, Pietzel didn't ask a lot of questions and would do just about anything requested by the doctor.

Following the disappearance of the Williams sisters, Holmes and Pietzel concocted an insurance fraud scheme they were sure couldn't fail. First, Holmes would take out a $10,000 policy from the Fidelity Mutual Life Association of Philadelphia in the name of B. F. Perry, a pseudonym used by Pietzel. Next, the two would acquire a cadaver, which they would disfigure in such a way as make it impossible to identify. They would work with a shady attorney they'd been told about who could confirm the victim's identity and collect the insurance money on behalf of B. F. Perry's widow, who just happened to be Mrs. Benjamin Pietzel. In the end, they would split the proceeds.

Unfortunately for Pietzel, Holmes had a Machiavellian double-cross in mind. In his confession Holmes admitted he had presented Pietzel with forged letters allegedly written by his wife that indicated she was unhappy with him. As a result, the insecure Pietzel began to drink heavily.

Holmes waited until Pietzel had passed out and then tied him up. "I proceeded to burn him alive by saturating his clothing and his face with benzene and igniting it with a match," Holmes wrote.

After Pietzel was dead, Holmes untied him and poured chloroform into the dead man's stomach so it would appear he had died from an accidental explosion of cleaning fluid.

The scam worked at first, and Holmes collected the insurance money. However, a convict named Marion Hedgeperth, who had once shared a cell with Holmes in St. Louis (where Holmes had been arrested for a short time for his involvement in a horse swindle that went wrong), decided to contact the insurance company after reading about the death of B. F. Perry. Hedgeperth had provided Holmes with the name of the attorney who assisted him with the plan and was promised a $500 commission. Having realized he was not going to get his share from Holmes, Hedgeperth informed the insurance company that the Perry death was suspiciously similar to a scheme he'd heard Holmes talk about in jail.

It was at this point that Holmes's carefully constructed house of lies began to crumble. The insurance company hired the Pinkerton National Detective Agency to find the doctor, and they picked him up in Boston. He confessed to the crime of insurance fraud and was extradited to Philadelphia.

While Holmes was in jail, police learned that in the months before he was picked up he had been traveling around the country with three of Benjamin Pietzel's children, who were now missing. Additionally, police began to realize that the body of B. F. Perry was actually Benjamin Pietzel.

"The charge of swindling may not be the only one Holmes will have to answer, for the more serious crime of murder may be laid to him," reported the *New York Times* on November 19, 1894. "The theory is advanced that the body found was really that of Pietzel and not of any one else."

Holmes began spinning fast. He told police that Pietzel had committed suicide and he arranged the scene so that it would appear it was an accident so he could collect the insurance money. He also said he had entrusted the three Pietzel children to a good friend, Minnie Williams, who had taken them to England.

It was all part of an elaborate charade. After killing Pietzel, Holmes had persuaded Mrs. Pietzel to let the children travel with him by claiming he was going to reunite them with their father, who he said was hiding out because of the insurance fraud.

He then convinced Mrs. Pietzel to follow, along with her other two children, again promising to unite the family in a safe location.

For the next several weeks, Holmes rented up to three houses simultaneously in various communities (primarily in the Midwest and East as well as Canada), in which resided the three Pietzel children, Mrs. Pietzel and her two other children, and he and his new wife, twenty-three-year-old Georgiana Yoke, who apparently had no idea what her husband was doing (at the time he was also still legally married to Clara Lovering and not-so-legally to Myrta Belnap). In one city Mrs. Pietzel's house was only four blocks from the house where her children were staying.

According to Erik Larson, Holmes was playing a twisted game. "He possessed them all and reveled in his possession," he wrote.

In June 1895, Detective Frank Geyer of Philadelphia was assigned to find the Pietzel children. After interviewing Holmes, who he thought was a bit slick, he embarked on a tedious three-week slog to retrace Holmes's every step with the children.

Guiding him was a packet of letters that police had found in a tin box that was with Holmes when he was arrested. The letters were written by the children to their mother but never mailed.

Based on the information contained in the letters, Geyer traveled from St. Louis to Cincinnati to Indianapolis to Detroit to Toronto. A tip led them to a house in the last city, where

Geyer discovered the bodies of two of the three children buried in a basement.

Holmes later confessed that he had locked the two girls in a trunk, which he pumped full of gas. Following a hunch, Geyer returned to Indianapolis—the last place where the other child was known to be—and continued his quest. After pursuing hundreds of leads, he found a rental agent who had rented a property to Holmes.

In the base of the home's chimney flue, Geyer uncovered teeth, a piece of a jawbone, and charred organs—the remains of the third Pietzel child.

While Geyer was searching for the Pietzel children, Chicago police, who previously had paid no attention to Holmes, opened up his castle to take a look. What they found was horrifying. Chicago newspapers soon offered lengthy stories with large headlines that blared: "Victims of A Fiend"; "No Jekyll, All Hyde"; and "Modern Bluebeard: H. H. Holmes' Castle Reveals His True Character."

The articles offered detailed floor plans of the strange building, including the trap doors, bewitching hallways, underground crematory, and "asphyxiation chamber." Articles speculated on the number of those murdered by Holmes in what the *Chicago Tribune* called his "veritable murder factory."

"There are hundreds of people who went to Chicago to see the Fair and were never heard from again," the *Tribune* reported on August 18, 1895. "Did these visitors to the Fair, strangers to

Chicago, find their way to Holmes' castle in answer to delusive advertising sent out by him, never to return again?"

Not surprisingly, a day later someone torched Holmes's hotel. The *Tribune* reported that nearby residents heard three explosions followed by a tremendous fire that destroyed most of the building.

The loss of the castle, however, didn't have an impact on what was happening in Philadelphia, where prosecutors charged Holmes with the death of Benjamin Pietzel.

On October 28, 1895, Holmes was put on trial and five days later found guilty of first-degree murder. Following several unsuccessful appeals, he was sentenced to death by hanging.

Over the next few months, Holmes penned his "final" confession—now he admitted to killing twenty-seven people—and, according to the *Tribune*, "is taking a great interest in the preparations for his execution, and talks freely about his approaching death. He says he would like the executioners to exercise great care to prevent his choking to death, and has expressed a hope that when he drops the rope will break his neck."

On the morning of May 7, 1896, Holmes was led to gallows on the grounds of the Moyamensing Prison in Philadelphia. His final words, "Take your time: don't bungle it," were directed in jest at the prison's assistant superintendent, Alex Richard, who slipped the noose over his neck and tightened it.

At 10:13 a.m., Richard released the trap door and Holmes

was hanged. According to the *New York Times,* "The neck was not broken, and there were a few convulsive twitches of the limbs that continued for about ten minutes."

Fearful that his grave might be robbed, Holmes gave specific instructions for his burial. According to the *Times,* his body was taken to a vault in Holy Cross Cemetery near Philadelphia, where the bottom of his coffin was filled with cement and his body was laid into the mixture and then covered completely with more cement. After the cement dried, the coffin was lowered into an unmarked grave in the cemetery, which had also been filled with cement, then covered with even more cement.

Following Holmes's death, the castle was rebuilt albeit in

HOLMES' "CASTLE"   (63d St., Chicago, Ill)

This postcard shows the exterior of the notorious Murder Castle hotel.

CHICAGO HISTORY MUSEUM (ICHi-27827)

much diminished fashion. A 1937 *Chicago Tribune* article noted that it "bears little resemblance to its once awful grandeur. In ordinary light it is difficult to tell what its original color was. The soot and grime of several decades have blighted its old hues."

A year later the structure was sold to the US government, which tore it down in order to build a new post office (still standing today).

As for why Holmes committed his crimes, perhaps the answer lies in the words of the *Chicago Tribune,* which said of him on the day after his execution: "Avarice undoubtedly was the mainspring of all his acts, but an avarice so inconceivably inhuman that it bred a contempt for the laws of man and God, and made murder a mere incident in his schemes."

So true.

BIBLIOGRAPHY

CHAPTER 1: THE GASMAN COMETH

"Anesthetic Prowler Adds Victim," *Mattoon Daily Journal-Gazette,* September 6, 1944.

"Anesthetic Prowler on Loose," *Mattoon Daily Journal-Gazette,* September 2, 1944.

"Assail Police for Calling Gas Scare a 'Hoax,'" *Chicago Tribune,* September 14, 1944.

Bartholomew, Robert E., "Remembering the 'Mad Gasser' of Mattoon, Illinois," www.reall.org, April, 1999.

Bartholomew, Robert E. and Robert Ladendorf, "The Mad Gasser of Mattoon: How the Press Created an Imaginary Chemical Weapons Attack," *Skeptical Inquirer,* July/August 2002.

"FBI at Mattoon as Gas Prowler Attacks 5 More," *Chicago Tribune,* September 10, 1944.

"'Gas Calls' at Vanishing Point," *Mattoon Daily Journal-Gazette,* September 13, 1944.

"Gas Spraying Phantom Hits 2 More Homes," *Chicago Tribune,* September 11, 1944.

"Illinois Gas Prowler Foils Police; Adds 13 Victims," *Miami News,* September 9, 1944.

"Illinois Town Seeking 'Poison Spray' Prowler," *St. Petersburg Times,* September 7, 1944.

"Intensify Hunt for Paralysis Gas Prowler," *Chicago Tribune,* September 7, 1944.

Johnson, Donald M., "The 'Phantom Anesthetist' of Mattoon: A Field Study of Mass Hysteria," *Journal of Abnormal and Social Psychology,* January 1945.

"Many Prowler Reports; Few Real," *Mattoon Daily Journal-Gazette,* September 11, 1944.

Maruna, Scott, *The Mad Gasser of Mattoon: Dispelling the Hysteria,* Swamp Gas Book Co., Jacksonville, IL, 2003.

"Mattoon Fiend Fells Two More With Poison Gas," *Chicago Tribune,* September 8, 1944.

"Mattoon's 'Gas' Attacks Called Mass Hysteria," *Chicago Tribune,* September 13, 1944.

"Mattoon's Gas Fiend Attacks Girl, 11, At Home," *Chicago Tribune,* September 9, 1944.

"Say 'Mattoon Madman' May Be Imaginary," *Berkeley Daily Gazette,* September 8, 1944.

"Secret Police to Hunt 'Facts' in Gas Mystery," *Chicago Tribune,* September 15, 1944.

CHAPTER 2: BIG BIRD ON THE LOOSE

"'Big Bird' flies south, couple says," *Chicago Tribune,* August 15, 1977.

"Big Birds Leave Ample Evidence of Their Size," *Chicago Tribune,* August 1, 1977.

Clark, Jerome and Loren Coleman, *The Unidentified & Creatures of the Outer Edge: The Early Works of Jerome Clark and Loren Coleman,* Anomalist Books, San Antonio/New York, 2006.

Coleman, Loren, *Mothman and Other Curious Encounters,* Paraview Books, New York, 2002.

Hall, Mark A., *Thunderbirds: America's Living Legends of Giant Birds,* Paraview Books, New York, 2004.

Temple, Wayne C., "The Piasá Bird: Fact or Fiction?," *Journal of the Illinois State Historical Society,* Autumn 1956.

"Witnesses Say Huge Black Birds Attacked Children While At Play," *The Hour,* Norwalk, CT, August 2, 1977.

CHAPTER 3: MACOMB'S FIREBUG

"Barn Burns At Scene of Many Mystery Fires," *Macomb Daily Journal,* August 17, 1948.

"Blazes Break Out in New Willey Home," *Macomb Daily Journal,* August 28, 1948.

Bord, Janet and Colin, *Unexplained Mysteries of the 20th Century,* Contemporary Books, Chicago, 1989.

"Fire Flares in Milk House at Willey Farm," *Macomb Daily Journal,* August 18, 1948.

Gaddis, Vincent H., *Mysterious Fires and Lights,* Dell Publishing Co., New York, 1967.

"Girl, 12, Confesses Setting 100 Fires at Farm Home," *Chicago Tribune,* August 31, 1948.

"'Mystery Fire' Burns Willey Farm House," *Macomb Daily Journal,* August 13, 1948.

"Phantom Fires Hit Two More Times at Farm," *Macomb Daily Journal,* August 19, 1948.

"Second Willey Barn Burns; Sabotage Test By Foreign Power Suspected By Expert," *Macomb Daily Journal,* August 20, 1948.

"Set Fires, Wanted to Go Live With Mother Girl, 13, Confesses," *Macomb Daily Journal,* August 30, 1948.

"Some Person Set Fires, Says Chicago Expert," *Macomb Daily Journal,* August 23, 1948.

"Suspect Arson in Farm Fires; Plan Hearing," *Macomb Daily Journal,* August 23, 1948.

"13-year-old Girl Center of Strange Fires," *Macomb Journal,* October 30, 1998.

"Willeys Still Baffled By Series of Blazes," *Macomb Daily Journal,* August 16, 1948.

"Willeys Still the Center of Wide Interest," *Macomb Daily Journal,* August 21, 1948.

"Willeys Worried By Fires But 'Not Afraid,'" *Macomb Daily Journal,* August 20, 1948.

"Wonet May Be Placed With Grandparents," *Macomb Daily Journal,* September 1, 1948.

"Wonet, 'Nice Kid Caught in Middle' By Family Mixup, Divorce," *Macomb Daily Journal,* August 31, 1948.

CHAPTER 4: TRAGEDY IN THE SUBURBS

"Barefoot Man Key in Percy Case," *Chicago Tribune,* September 18, 1967.

"Bayonet Is Percy Clew," *Chicago Tribune,* September 23, 1966.

"Believe Killer Knew Home of Victim," *Chicago Tribune,* September 19, 1966.

"4 Months Give No New Percy Murder Clew," *Chicago Tribune,* December 19, 1966.

Goudie, Chuck, "Percy Killing: The Forty Year File," WLS-TV website, http://abclocal.go.com/wls/ story?section=news&id=4563621.

Goudie, Chuck, "Questions about Valerie Percy Murder Outlive Her Father," *Daily Herald* (Arlington Heights, IL), September 18, 2011.

Lindberg, Richard, *Return to the Scene of the Crime: A Guide to Infamous Places in Chicago,* Cumberland House Publishing, Nashville, TN, 1999.

"Mrs. Percy's Murder Story," *Chicago Tribune,* October 14, 1966.

Murray, David, *Charles Percy of Illinois,* Harper & Row, New York, 1968.

"Mystery, Memories Linger After Demolition of Former Percy Home," *Chicago Tribune,* June 4, 2010.

"Newly Disclosed Account Surfaces in 1966 Valerie Percy Murder Case," *Chicago Tribune,* June 14, 2011.

"News of Death Shocks College Friends," *Chicago Tribune,* September 19, 1966.

"Percy's Daughter Slain!," *Chicago Tribune,* September 18, 1966.

"Percy Decides He'll Sell 17-Room Home," *Chicago Tribune,* November 21, 1966.

"Percy Doctor Says Slayer is a Madman," *Chicago Tribune,* September 20, 1966.

"Percy Girl Slain By Thief," *The Miami News,* November 26, 1973.

"Percy Killer Described," *Chicago Tribune,* September 20, 1966.

"Percy Last to See Twin Until Attack," *Chicago Tribune,* September 28, 1966.

"Percy Murder Case Figure is Sentenced," *Chicago Tribune,* January 3, 1970.

"Percy Murder Site Tied to Burglar Ring," *The Telegraph Herald* (Dubuque, IA), December 27, 1973.

"Percy Murder Still Puzzle," *Chicago Tribune,* September 14, 1972.

"Percy Slaying Still Remains Unsolved," *Chicago Tribune,* September 16, 1968.

"Percys Leave Scene of Tragedy," *Chicago Tribune,* September 22, 1966.

"Psychiatrist Says Killer Acted in Rage," *Chicago Tribune,* September 20, 1966.

Rasmussen, William T., *Corroborating Evidence III: A True Crime Story,* Sunstone Press, Santa Fe, NM, 2011.

"Tip Leads Reporter to Valerie Percy's Killer," *Harlan Daily Enterprise* (KY), March 4, 1977.

"2 Gangsters Named as Valerie Percy Killers," *Chicago Tribune,* November 25, 1973.

"2 Probers Still Look for Valerie's Killer," *Chicago Tribune,* September 14, 1969.

CHAPTER 5: BURNING MYSTERIES

Arnold, Larry E., *The Mysterious Fires of Ablaze! Spontaneous Human Combustion,* M. Evans & Company, Lanham, MD, 1995.

Christiansen, Jo-Anne, *Ghost Stories of Illinois,* Lone Pine Publishing, Edmonton, Canada, 2000.

Overton, James, M.D., "On the Causes of Spontaneous Human Combustion," *The Boston Medical and Surgical Journal,* October 14, 1835.

"Mysterious Burns Fatal to Janitor of Bloomington Bank," *Chicago Tribune,* September 8, 1949.

CHAPTER 6: MARY, MARY, QUITE CONTRARY

Bielski, Ursula, *Chicago Haunts: Ghostlore of the Windy City,* Lake Claremont Press, Chicago, 1998.

Bill Geist column, *Suburban Trib,* January 31, 1979.

"Free Spirits Who Hunt Ghosts for Fun and Profit," *Chicago Tribune,* September 6, 1984.

"Halloween Haunts," *Chicago Sun-Times,* October 26, 2000.

"Haunting a Ghost Named Mary," *Chicago Tribune,* October 31, 1974.

"History Makes City a Ghost Hunter's Dream, er, Nightmare," *Chicago Tribune,* June 13, 1986.

Johnson, Ray, "Resurrection Mary," www.hauntdetective.com.

Kaczmarek, Dale, *Windy City Ghosts: The Haunted History of Chicago,* Whitechapel Productions Press, Alton, IL, 2000.

"Patch Spends Five Minutes with Richard T. Crowe," Oak Lawn Patch, www.oaklawn.patch.com, November 30, 2010.

"Resurrection Mary Still Wanders Amid the Myths on Frightful Nights," *Chicago Tribune,* October 25, 1992.

"Seeing is Believing: Willowbrook Ballroom Will Be Forever Linked to the Ghost Called 'Resurrection Mary,'" *Chicago Sun-Times,* October 26, 2003.

Selzer, Adam, "Resurrection Mary," www.chicagounbelievable .com, October 20, 2008.

"Some of Chicago's Favorite Haunts," *Chicago Tribune,* May 13, 1974.

Taylor, Troy, *Haunted Chicago: History & Hauntings of the Windy City,* Whitechapel Productions Press, Alton, IL, 2003.

CHAPTER 7: THE HORROR

Coleman, Loren, "Enfield Monster Memories + Murder," www.cryptomundo.com.

"'It's Something That's There'—Monster Lurks Along Wabash," *Coschocton* (OH) *Tribune,* May 7, 1973.

Miller, David L., Kenneth J. Mietus, and Richard A. Mathers, "A Critical Examination of the Social Contagion Image of

Collective Behavior: The Case of the Enfield Monster," *The Sociological Quarterly,* Winter 1978.

"Scientists Still in the Search for 'Big Foot,'" *Boca Raton News,* December 23, 1973.

"Wabash 'Monster' Being Sought," *Robinson Daily News,* May 12, 1973.

CHAPTER 8: ACCIDENTAL SHOOTING OR ASSASSINATION?

"Assassin Faces Court Today; Spurns Lawyer," *Chicago Tribune,* February 17, 1933.

"Assassin in Jail, Tells of His Motives," *Chicago Tribune,* February 16, 1933.

"Chicago Woman Witnesses Shooting; Tells Details," *Chicago Tribune,* February 16, 1933.

Collins, Max Allan, *True Detective,* St. Martin's Press, New York, 1983.

"Death Takes Mayor Cermak," *Chicago Tribune,* March 6, 1933.

Eghigian, Mars, *After Capone,* Cumberland House Publishing, Nashville, TN, 2006.

Humble, Ronald D., *Frank Nitti: The True Story of Chicago's Notorious Enforcer,* Barricade Books, Fort Lee, NJ, 2007.

Information released by the Federal Bureau of Investigation under the Freedom of Information Act, http://digital.library .miami.edu/gov/FDRAssn.html.

"Maniac Fires on Roosevelt; Cermak Shot; Wound Grave," *Chicago Tribune,* February 16, 1933.

Picchi, Blaise, *The Five Weeks of Giuseppe Zangara,* Academy Chicago Publishers, Chicago, 1998.

Russo, Gus, *The Outfit,* Bloomsbury USA, New York, 2003.

Schoenberg, Robert J., *Mr. Capone: The Real—and Complete— Story of Al Capone,* William Morrow, New York, 1993.

"Slayer of Cermak Will Die Today," *Chicago Tribune,* March 20, 1933.

Tuohy, John William, "The Guns of Zangara, Parts 1–3," Rick Porrello's American Mafia.com, www.americanmafia.com, retrieved March 19, 2011.

"Zangara Dies for Murder of Mayor Cermak," *Chicago Tribune,* March 21, 1933.

CHAPTER 9: POSSESSION IN WATSEKA

Stevens, E. Winchester, *The Watseka Wonder,* Religio-Philosophical Publishing House, Chicago, 1878.

Tymn, Michael E., "The Watseka Wonder," Academy of Spirituality and Paranormal Studies, Inc., www.aspsi.org.

CHAPTER 10: INVASION OF THE PHANTOM GASBAGS

"Airship Headed For Chicago," *Chicago Tribune,* April 4, 1897.

"Air Ship Here Again," *Chicago Times-Herald,* April 11, 1897.

"Air Ship is Seen in Illinois," *Chicago Times-Herald,* April 6, 1897.

"'Air Ship' is Speedy: Covers Vast Area of Ground," *Chicago Times-Herald,* April 13, 1897.

"Airship Myth Yet Soars," *Chicago Tribune,* April 12, 1897.

"Air Ship Now Seen at Evanston," *Chicago Times-Herald,* April 4, 1897.

"Airship Passes Over Chicago," *Chicago Tribune,* April 11, 1897.

"Air Ship Seen Near Minonk, Ill.," *Chicago Times-Herald,* April 17, 1897.

"The Apparition of the Air," *San Francisco Call,* November 24, 1896.

Busby, Michael, *Solving the 1897 Airship Mystery,* Pelican Publishing, Gretna, LA, 2004.

"California Airship on the Wing," *Chicago Tribune,* April 11, 1897.

Clark, Jerome, *Hidden Realms, Lost Civilizations, and Beings From Other Worlds,* Visible Ink Press, Canton, MI, 2010.

Cohen, Daniel, *The Great Airship Mystery,* Dodd, Mead & Company, New York, 1981.

"Edison Scoffs At The Airship," *Chicago Tribune,* April 20, 1897.

"A Genuine Aerial Ship," *Sacramento Daily Record-Union* (CA), November 23, 1896.

"Mission of the Aerial Ship," *San Francisco Call,* November 25, 1896.

"Mystery of the Sky: 'Air Ship' Seen By Thousands," *Chicago Times-Herald,* April 10, 1897.

Rath, Jay, *The I-Files: True Reports of Unexplained Phenomena in Illinois,* Trail Books, Boulder, CO, 1999.

"Saw the Mystic Flying Light," *San Francisco Call,* November 22, 1896.

"See Airship Or A Star," *Chicago Tribune,* April 10, 1897.

"Sees Man Fishing From Air Ship," *Chicago Tribune,* April 16, 1897.

"Snapshot of Air Ship," *Chicago Times-Herald,* April 12, 1897.

"Strange Craft of the Sky," *San Francisco Call,* November 19, 1896.

"That Mysterious Light," *Sacramento Daily Record-Union* (CA), November 19, 1896.

"That Peculiar Night Visitant," *San Francisco Call,* November 20, 1896.

"They Claim They Saw a Flying Airship," *San Francisco Call,* November 18, 1896.

"Three Airships, Says Hart," *San Francisco Call,* November 29, 1896.

"What Was It!," *Sacramento Daily Record-Union* (CA), November 18, 1896.

"A Winged Ship in the Sky," *San Francisco Call,* November 23, 1896.

CHAPTER 11: DID ANYONE REALLY STARVE ON STARVED ROCK?

Baldwin, Elmer, *History of La Salle County, Illinois,* Rand McNally & Co., Chicago, 1877.

"Fort Rock," *The National Magazine,* 1855.

"Illinois Indians. The Siege of Starved Rock, Near Ottawa," *New York Times,* May 5, 1872.

Osman, Eaton G., *Starved Rock: A Chapter of Colonial History,* A. Flanagan Company, Chicago, 1895.

Roundy, William Noble, *The Last of the Illini or The Legend of Starved Rock, A Tale of Illinois,* Hack & Anderson, Chicago, 1916.

"Starved Rock Monument," *The Newburgh Telegram,* July 13, 1912.

Walczynski, Mark, "The Starved Rock Massacre of 1769: Fact or Fiction," *Journal of the Illinois State Historical Society,* Fall 2007.

CHAPTER 12: THE NEW MONSTER OF THE MIDWAY

"Couple See Man-Sized Bird . . . Creature . . . Something," *Point Pleasant Gazette* (WV), November 16, 1966.

"Eight People Say They Saw 'Creature,'" *Williamson Daily News* (WV), November 18, 1966.

"Is Mysterious Creature Balloon or Crane?," *Athens Messenger* (OH), November 26, 1966.

Keel, John A., *The Mothman Prophecies,* Tor Books, New York, 2002.

"Monster Bird With Red Eyes May Be Crane," *Gettysburg Times* (PA), December 1, 1966.

"Monster No Joke For Those Who Saw It," *Athens Messenger* (OH), November 18, 1966.

Mothmen website, www.mothmen.us.

"A Possible Mothman Sighting in Chicago, Illinois?" www .meetstheweird.com, September 30, 2011.

"2nd Mothman/Bat-Like Object Witnessed Over Chicago," www.naturalplane.blogspot.com, October 13, 2011.

Taylor, Troy, "Mothman: The Enigma of Point Pleasant," www.prairieghosts.com.

"3rd Mothman/Bat-Like Object Reported Over Chicago," www.naturalplane.blogspot.com, October 14, 2011.

"Winged, Red-Eyed 'Thing' Chases Point Couples Across Countryside," *Athens Messenger* (OH), November 17, 1966.

CHAPTER 13: VIRGIL BALL'S OBSESSION

"Cave-in Halts Search for Illinois Man," *Telegraph-Herald* (Dubuque, IA), August 2, 1957.

"Farmington Students Resurrect the Rawley Story," *Daily Ledger* (Canton, IL), November 8, 2003.

"Mystery Remains Unsolved To This Day," *Peoria Journal-Star,* November 6, 2000.

"New Clue Indicates Car Dumped into Old Mine," *Telegraph-Herald* (Dubuque, IA), August 2, 1957.

"Science Enlisted in Search for Missing Land Operator," *Chicago Tribune,* April 24, 1955.

"Sheriff Hopes to Find Body," *Telegraph-Herald* (Dubuque, IA), August 2, 1957.

"Sheriff Was Known for Dedication: Fulton County's Virgil Ball Dies at 85," *Peoria Journal-Star,* June 2, 1999.

"Whatever Happened to Fay Rawley?," *Peoria Journal-Star*, February 12, 2001.

"Where is Fay Rawley (and His Cadillac)," *The Zephyr* (Galesburg, IL), August 6, 1998.

CHAPTER 14: THE DIABOLICAL DR. HOLMES

"Autobiography of an Arch Murderer," *Chicago Tribune*, April 11, 1896.

Borowski, John, *The Strange Case of Dr. H. H. Holmes: World's Fair Serial Killer*, Waterfront Productions, West Hollywood, CA, 2005.

"Career of Holmes, the Swindler," *Chicago Tribune*, November 25, 1894.

"End of the Holmes Case," *Chicago Tribune*, May 8, 1896.

"Fired For a Purpose," *Chicago Tribune*, August 20, 1895.

"Holmes' Confession," *Philadelphia North American*, April 11, 1896.

"Holmes Cool to the End," *New York Times*, May 6, 1896.

"Holmes Den Burned," *Chicago Tribune*, August 19, 1895.

"Holmes Fears Hatch," *New York Times*, August 2, 1895.

"Holmes Gives Up Hope: Multimurderer Now Gloomily Awaits His Execution," *Chicago Tribune*, May 3, 1896.

"Holmes Gives a Written Interview: He Attempts to Explain Some of the Mysteries in His Case," *Chicago Tribune,* August 2, 1895.

"Holmes Hears His Fate," *Chicago Tribune,* December 1, 1895.

Holmes, H. H., *Holmes' Own Story,* Burk & McFetridge Co., Philadelphia, 1895.

"Holmes Murder Castle Razed for Post Office," *Chicago Tribune,* May 15, 1938.

"Holmes Sentenced to Die," *New York Times,* December 1, 1895.

"Holmes to Be Hanged May 7," *Chicago Tribune,* March 6, 1896.

Larson, Erik, *The Devil in the White City,* Vintage Books, New York, 2003.

Martin, John Barlow, "The Master of the Murder Castle: A Classic Chicago Crime," *Harpers,* December 1943.

"May Be Charged With Murder," *New York Times,* November 19, 1894.

"Modern Bluebeard: H. H. Holmes Castles Reveals His True Character," *Chicago Tribune,* August 18, 1895.

"Murder Castle! Record of H. H. Holmes Sensational Crimes," *Chicago Tribune,* March 21, 1937.

"No Jekyll, All Hyde," *Chicago Tribune,* July 29, 1895.

"Pietzel Children Found," *New York Times,* July 16, 1895.

Spikol, Liz, "Holmes Sweet Holmes," *Philadelphia Weekly,*
    October 29, 2003.

"Spins His Own Web," *Chicago Tribune,* November 22, 1895.

"Two More Victims," *Chicago Tribune,* July 21, 1895.

"Victims of a Fiend," *Chicago Tribune,* July 20, 1895.

INDEX

A

Acquilano, Nelson, 54–55
Ahern, John J., 35
airships, 111–24
Alinsky, Saul, 98
Alter, Minerva, 105–6, 109
Alton (IL), 15, 23, 24, 25–26
Armstrong, Perry, 129–30
Arnold, Larry E., 59
Astoria (IL), 118–20
Aurora (TX), 123

B

Baldwin, Elmer, 130
Ball, John, 147
Ball, Virgil, 146, 147–53, 155–
    56, 157
Beecher, William, 21
Belnap, Myrta, 163, 164, 170
Bence, Bertha, 10
Bennett, C. W., 31
Bielski, Ursula, 73–75
Binning, George, 108
Bloomington (IL), 61–63, 84
Blue Creek (WV), 141
Bolingbrook (IL), 63–64
Bonnie (IL), 83
Booth, Oscar D., 121–22

Bord, Colin, 64
Bord, Janet, 64
Bowler, James, 91
Bregovy, Mary, 75
Bruce, Henry Addington,
    109, 110
Buell, M. B., 148
Burgard, John, 32, 36–38
Burner, Irene, 34
Busby, Michael, 123–24

C

Cairo (IL), 15
Callison, Grant, 16–17
Callison, Wilma, 16
Carlinville (IL), 119
Caton, John Dean, 127–29
Cermak, Anton, 86–87, 90–91,
    94–95, 96, 97, 98
Chappell, John, 20–21
Chappell, Wanda, 20–21
Chassagnoil, M., 55–56
Chet's Melody Lounge, 72, 76
Chicago, 117–18, 121–22, 137–
    39, 143, 145, 158, 163–68,
    171–74
Cigrand, Emeline, 166
Clark, Jerome, 83, 85

Clendenen, Floyd, 58–59
Clinton, A. C., 121
Clinton, Charles, 121–22
Cole, C. E., 1–2, 8, 11
Coleman, E. M., 16
Coleman, Loren, 15, 16,
    82–83, 85
Collins, C. E., 94
Collins, George D., 114–15
Connor, Julia, 165–66
Connor, Ned, 165
Connor, Pearl, 165, 166
Cordes, Beulah, 6–7, 9–10
Cordes, Carl, 6–7
Crowe, Richard T., 66, 76
Curtis, Edward S., 17

D
Daley, Robert P., 49–50
Daniels, James, 18, 19
dead, communicating with the,
    99–110
deaths, 41–53, 54–64, 86–98,
    146–57, 158–74
Demorest, J. J., 42
Douglas, Paul, 41, 42, 48, 49
Driskell, Ramona, 9
Driskell, Violet, 9
Duncan, Kenneth, 141

E
Eagle, Leona, 28, 39
Edison, Thomas, 119–20
Elgin (IL), 145
Enfield (IL), 77–82, 84–85
Enfield Horror, 77–85

Evans, Harold James, 50, 51
Evanston (IL), 116, 117

F
Farmer City (IL), 84
fires, 27–40, 54–64
Forcade, Herbert, 25
Fort St. Louis, 126
Fox Indians, 125, 127, 134–36
Franquelin, Jean-Baptiste-
    Louis, 23
Fulton County (IL), 146–57

G
Galesburg (IL), 16–17
Garett, Gary, 77, 78, 81
gas, paralyzing, 1–13
Gautier, Redmond, 90
Geist, Bill, 70–71
Geyer, Frank, 170–71
ghost story, 65–76
Goodwin, Travis, 17–18
Graham, Edna, 50
Graham, William, 50
Gust, Louis C., 33–34

H
Hall, Mark, 15, 18, 21, 23, 26
Harlow's (nightclub), 69–70
Harmar, Max L., 120–21
Harpole, Lepton, 83
Hart, William H. H., 115
Hedgeperth, Marion, 168–69
Henry, James, 15
hitchhiking ghost story, 65–76
Hodgson, Richard, 109
Hohf, Robert, 43, 47

Hohimer, Frank, 51–52
Hohimer, Wayne, 51
Holmes, Henry Howard, 158–74
Holton, E. S., 163
Holton, Mrs. E. S., 163
Huffer, "Texas John," 19–20

I
Illinois Indians, 125, 126–33,
    134–36
Imlay, Bill, 152

J
Johnson, Daisy, 39
Johnson, Donald M., 2
Johnson, George, 141
Junkin, Laura, 7
Justice (IL), 65–76

K
Kaczmarek, Dale, 69
Kaskaskia Indians, 125–26
Kearney, Aline, 2–5
Kearney, Dorothy, 2–3
Kearney, Mr., 4
Keel, John A., 142, 144–45
Kelleher, Edward J., 43
Kenilworth (IL), 41, 42–52
Key Mine, 147–53

L
Lacon (IL), 22
Ladendorf, Robert, 13
Larson, Eric, 160–61, 164,
    165, 170
Larson, John, 56–57, 61
La Salle, René-Robert Cavelier,
    Sieur de, 126

*Last of the Illini or The Legend
    of Starved Rock* (Roundy),
    130–32
Lawndale (IL), 17–19
Lewis, C. S., 13
Llewellyn, Farley, 11–13
Logan County (IL), 19
Lovering, Clara A., 63–164,
    162, 170
Lowe, Marlon, 17–19, 21
Lowe, Ruth, 18–19
Lyle, John, 97

M
Macomb (IL), 27–40
Mad Gasser of Mattoon, The
    (Maruna), 5–6, 7, 11–13
Main, Bob, 69–70
Malchow, Frederick J., 50–51
Mallette, Steve, 140
Marquette, Jacques, 22–23,
    26, 125
Martin, Bernadine, 151–52
Maruna, Scott, 5–6, 7,
    11–13, 22
Mathers, Richard A., 79–82
Mattoon (IL), 1–13
McCann, Walter, 118
McDaniel, Henry, 78–80, 81,
    84–85
McNeil, Arthur, 28
McNeil, Arthur, Jr., 28, 33
McNeil, Wonet, 33, 36–39, 40
Meachelle (Potawatomi
    chief), 127
Mietus, Kenneth J., 79–82

Miller, David L., 79–82
Miskowski, Mary, 75–76
monsters, 14–26, 77–85, 137–45
Mothman, 137–45
Mothman Prophecies, The (film), 139–40, 142
Mount Vernon (IL), 83
murders, 41–53, 158–74
Murphy, Michael, 56, 57
Murray, David, 48

N
Nashville (IL), 117
Native American lore, 14–15, 17. *See also specific tribes*
Nitti, Frank, 86, 96
Norkus, Anna Marija, 73–75
Norkus, August, 74

O
Oczki, Beatrice, 63–64
Odin (IL), 20–21
O'Donnell, Joseph, 122
Oh Henry Ballroom, 73, 74
Osman, Eaton, 132
Osman, William, Jr., 132
Ottawa Indians, 125, 127–28, 129–32
Ouashala (Fox chief), 134–35

P
Palus, Jerry, 66
Parker, Mrs. (mother of Nellie), 106
Parker, Nellie, 106
Parkinson, Charlie, 153, 154–56

Partridge, Newell, 141–42
Peoria Indians, 125, 134–36
Percy, Charles, 41–42, 44, 46–47, 48–49, 50, 52
Percy, Loraine, 45–46, 50
Percy, Sharon, 43–44
Percy, Valerie, 41, 42–52
Perry, B. F., 167–68, 169
Phillips, Ed, 79
Piasá, 22–26
Pietzel, Benjamin, 167–68, 169, 172
Pietzel, Mrs. Benjamin, 168, 169–70
Piper, Richard T., 9–10
Point Pleasant (WV), 140–41, 144–45
Pontiac (Ottawa chief), 127
Potawatomi Indians, 125, 127–28, 129–32
Price, Robert, 16
Prusinski, Richard, 76

R
Raef, Mr. and Mrs. Urban, 5
Rainbow, Rick, 80
Ralph (cab driver), 70–71
Rath, Jay, 122
Rawley, Fay, 146–57
Rawley, Hazel, 147, 154
Rawley, Robert, 154, 155
Reedy, Martha, 3–4
Resurrection Mary, 65–76
Richard, Alex, 172–73
Rider, Ann Marie, 5–6
Rider, Joe, 5–6

Rider, Mrs. Charles, 5–6
Robertson, Mrs. Earl, 3–4
Rock Island (IL), 117
Roff, Ann, 105–6
Roff, Asa, 101–2, 104, 105, 108, 109, 110, 111
Roff, Mary, 102, 103, 105, 106–8, 109, 110
Roff House, 110
Rooney, Matilda, 54, 56–60
Rooney, Patrick, 56, 57, 61
Roosevelt, Franklin D., 86, 87, 89–94, 96–98
Roundy, William Noble, 130–32
Rugendorf, Leo, 51, 52
Russell, John, 23–25, 26
Russo, Gus, 97–98

S
Sacramento (CA), 112–13
Samsell, John, 141
Scarberry, Roger, 140
Schoolcroft, Henry, 130
Seneca (IL), 54, 56–60
serial killer, 158–74
Sheets, Tom, 22
Shelbyville, Lake, 20
Shick-Shack (Ottawa chief), 129–30
shooting death, 86–98
Sigmund, Walter F., 15
Silver Bridge, 144–45
Simpkins, Opal, 39
Singh, A. G., 34–35
Sinnott, William, 98

Sloman, Sophie Schroeder, 38–39
Smith, Frances, 8–9
Smith, Maxine, 8–9
spirit possession, 99–110
spontaneous human combustion, 54–64
Springfield (IL), 22
Starved Rock, 125–36
Stevens, E. Winchester, 99–101, 102–3, 104–6, 107–8, 110
Stoneking, Walter, 28, 29
Summum (IL), 146–57

T
Taylor, Troy, 69, 72
Temple, Wayne C., 23, 25–26
Texas, 122–23
Thompson, Jim, 34
Thompson, Oly O., 95
thunderbirds, 14–22, 26
Tiskilwa (IL), 145
Toman, Andrew J., 45
Troyer, Aura, 61–63
Tuohy, John W., 96, 97

V
Vaudreuil, Pierre François de Rigaud, Marquis de, 135
Vennum, Mary Lurancy "Rancy," 96–110
Vennum, Thomas, 105

W
Wagner, Helen, 147, 154
Walczynski, Mark, 132–36

water witching, 152

Watseka (IL), 99–110

West Virginia, 139–42, 144–45

Wilcox, Mark, 98

Willey, Charles, 27–29, 31, 37, 39

Willey, Lou, 27–29, 30–31, 34, 35–36, 37

Williams, Anna, 167

Williams, Minnie, 162, 166–67, 169

Wilson, Fred, 35

Wright, Thomas V., 11

Y

Yoke, Georgiana, 170

Z

Zangara, Giuseppe, 86–98

Zangara, Salvatore, 87, 89

ABOUT THE AUTHOR

Richard Moreno is the author of thirteen books, including *Illinois Curiosities* and *It Happened in Illinois* for Globe Pequot Press. He currently serves as a journalism instructor and director of student publications at Western Illinois University. He resides in Macomb, Illinois, with his wife and family.